Geographical Skills

for A Level Years 1 & 2
for **Edexcel**

Garrett Nagle and Paul Guinness

Edited by: **Garrett Nagle**

informe

For Angela, Rosie, Patrick and Bethany

For Mary

© Anforme Ltd 2018
ISBN 978-1-78014-084-1
Images supplied by Shutterstock.com. All other attributed diagrams
and photographs used with permission from copyright holders.

Anforme Ltd, Stocksfield Hall, Stocksfield, Northumberland NE43 7TN.

Typeset by George Wishart & Associates, Whitley Bay.
Printed by Stephens & George Print Group, Merthyr Tydfil.

Contents

Chapter 1

Introduction

Geography is a subject that includes sciences as well as arts. It bridges the natural and social worlds – this is one of the reasons why Geography is so important – and unique. The different sub-sections of Geography (e.g. rivers, biogeography, urbanisation, globalisation) use different methods in their data collection and analysis.

In general, Physical Geography uses the 'scientific method' – the inductive process from observed and experimental methods. The scientific route to explanation includes the collection and measurement of data (quantification), followed by inductive generalisation, leading to scientific laws and theories. However, in reality, science and empirical observation (measurement) are rarely value-free or politically neutral – the debate over climate change, and the use of 'supporting data' by differing factions illustrates this. Nevertheless, this does not mean that the scientific approach has no validity – merely that it should be considered in relation to the aims, methods and values of those that are using it. In contrast, many Human Geographers make use of qualitative data – whereby meaning may be based on interpretation.

Quantitative data are those in which the data can be measured. In contrast, **qualitative data** are those that require other forms of description e.g. a newspaper article or a piece of art, which may illustrate some of the values (bias) of the author. Quantitative techniques include statistical, graphical, cartographic and ICT-techniques. Data is collected, analysed and presented, using a mixture of the above techniques. Qualitative techniques include interviews, textual and visual sources, creative- and social-media, photographs, sketches, newspaper articles and oral accounts.

Geography bridges the natural and social worlds

Primary data are those that you collect yourself. In contrast, **secondary data** are those that have already been published e.g. a map, a book/article/government data etc. Secondary data may be affected by the aims and methods of those collecting it, and so are rarely perfect for research purposes. In Physical Geography, one of the main sources of primary data is the measurement of the form (shape) of a feature e.g. a river or a sand dune system, whereas in Human Geography one of the most popular forms of primary data is a questionnaire or a land-use survey.

From your GCSE/IGCSE studies you will have built up a range of basic geographical skills in your study of geography prior to A-Level. The Edexcel specification identifies two main categories of skills, namely qualitative and quantitative skills, although these can be sub-divided into five categories of over-lapping skills which include:

- core skills.
- cartographic skills.
- graphical skills.
- statistical skills.
- ICT skills.

Core skills

The core skills include a wide range of graphical-, literacy- and numerical-skills. For example, there are:

- Use and annotation of illustrative and visual material: base maps, sketch maps, OS maps (at a variety of scales), diagrams, graphs, field sketches, photographs, geospatial, geo-located and digital imagery;
- Use of overlays, both physical and electronic;
- Literacy – use of factual text and discursive/creative material and coding techniques when analysing texts;
- Numeracy – use of number, measure and measurement; and
- Questionnaires and interview techniques.

Cartographic skills

For many people, cartographical (map) skills are the mark of the Geographer! These include:

- Atlas skills.
- Weather maps, including synoptic charts.
- Maps with located proportional symbols.
- Maps showing movement – flow lines, desire lines, and trip lines.
- Maps showing spatial patterns – choropleth, isolines and dot maps.

Graphical skills

There are a wide range of graphical skills including:

- Line graphs – including simple, comparative, compound and divergent.
- Bar graphs – including simple, comparative, compound and divergent.
- Scatter graphs, and the use of best fit lines.
- Pie charts and proportional divided circles.
- Triangular graphs.
- Graphs with logarithmic scales.
- Dispersion diagrams.
- Lorenz curves

Statistical skills

Statistical skills include:

- Measures of central tendency – mean, mode and median.
- Measures of dispersion – range, inter-quartile range and standard deviation.
- T-tests.
- Inferential and relational statistical techniques to include Spearman's Rank Correlation Coefficient and Chi-squared test and the application of significance tests.
- Gini coefficient.

ICT skills

Developments in ICT are occurring all the time, and you are expected to be able to:

- Use remotely sensed data.
- Use electronic databases.
- Use innovative sources of data such as crowd souring and 'big data', and,
- Use ICT to generate evidence of many of the skills such as producing maps, graphs and statistical calculations.

Data collection: sampling

It is impossible and impractical to measure everything. Thus, a sample is taken. A sample is a representative body of data which illustrates the characteristics of the total population. A large number of items (the total population) can be represented by a small sub-section (the sample). Sampling is therefore an efficient use of time and resources which make it possible to make statements about the total population by using a representative section. Sampling makes fieldwork investigations manageable.

There are different types of sampling which have their own strengths and weaknesses. In a general sense, there are two main types of sampling – **spatial** sampling and **temporal** sampling. Spatial sampling refers to samples that vary in where they are taken from. Temporal sampling refers to samples that are taken over different time periods. Both can be used – for example monitoring water quality changes above and below a sewage outlet between summer and winter.

Both types of sampling can be sub-divided into three main sub-types, **random**, **systematic** and **stratified** (Figure 1.1). Before selecting one or more types of sampling, a number of questions should be considered:

- What is the population being studied and in what area/time?

- What is the minimum size of sampling needed to produce reliable information and results?

- What is the most appropriate form of sampling for the enquiry?

Figure 1.1: Types of sampling

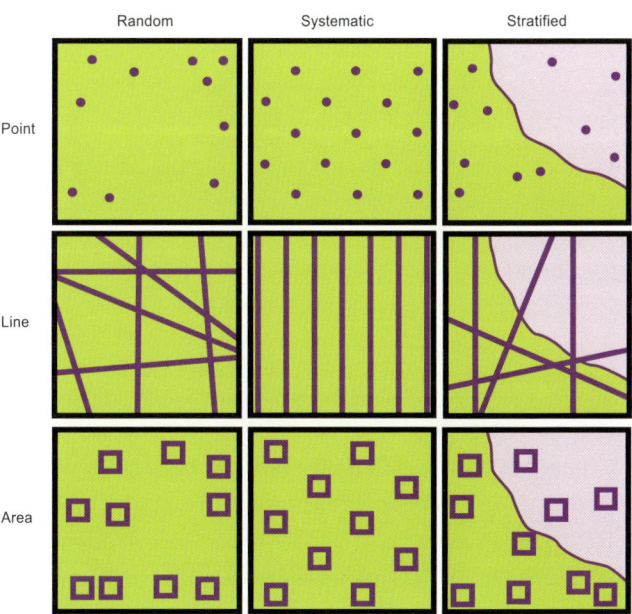

Random sampling

In a random sample, each item has an equal chance of being picked. Samples are often picked by using a random number table (Table 1.1). This is a table with no bias in the sequence of numbers. Once a number is chosen it can be related to a map, a grid reference, an angular direction and distance. Although fair, the random sample may miss important parts of the survey area. It is also very time consuming to do properly.

Table 1.1: A random number table

17	42	28	23	17	59	66	38	61	02	10	78
33	53	70	11	54	48	63	50	90	37	21	46
77	84	87	67	39	95	85	54	97	37	33	41
61	05	92	08	29	94	19	96	50	01	33	85
50	14	30	85	38	97	56	37	08	12	23	07
27	26	08	79	61	03	62	93	23	29	26	04
03	64	59	07	42	95	81	39	06	41	29	81
17	08	72	87	46	75	73	00	26	04	66	91
40	49	27	56	48	79	34	32	81	22	60	53

Systematic sampling

Systematic sampling is much quicker and easier than random sampling. Items are chosen at regular intervals e.g. every five metres, every tenth person, and so on. However, it is possible that a systematic sample will miss out important features. For example, in a survey of soil moisture and temperature in a ploughed field, if the surveys are taken on every ridge (or every furrow) and disregard other important microclimates, the results will be biased. The major problem with this type of sampling is that it can easily give a biased result because the sample is too small and as a result large areas are not included in the sample.

Stratified sampling

If it is known that there are important sub-groups in an area, for example different rock types which could influence soil types or farming types, it is possible to make a representative sample that takes into account all of the sub-groups in the study area. It is also possible to 'weight' the sample so that there is a proportionate number of samples related to the relative size of each sub-group.

Sample size

Determining the appropriate size of a sample is a critical matter. It depends on the nature and aims of the investigation but also on the time available (and other practical considerations such as access, land ownership, safety and so on). There are statistical formulae that can be used to determine sample size for a survey. Such statistical tests often depend on **confidence limits** i.e. statistical limits of probability that tell you how significant your results are likely to be. These are shown below in Table 1.2. For example, in a survey of vegetation in an area, with a sample 100 points and 90% of the points were seen to be occupied by deciduous woodland, the true figure (at the 95% confidence level) lies between 90% +/-6% i.e. between 96% and 84%. What is clear is that the larger the sample size the narrower the limits of the true population.

Confidence limits are based on normal probability. This assumes that 50% of the values are above the average (mean) and 50% are below the average. It also assumes that most of the values are within one standard deviation (see pages 65-67) of the mean. Probability states that in a normal distribution:

- 68% of samples lie within +/-1 standard deviation of the mean.

- 95% of samples lie within +/-2 standard deviations of the mean.

- 99.9% of samples lie within +/-3 standard deviations of the mean.

In other words, there is less than a 1 in 100 chance that the mean lies outside the sample mean +/-3 standard deviations, and less than a 1 in 20 chance that the true population mean lies outside the sample mean +/-2 standard deviations.

Table 1.2: Confidence levels and sample size

Range of error of estimates of population with one characteristic at 95% confidence limit

Percentage calculated	Sample size 25	Sample size 50	Sample size 100
98% or 2%	5.6	4	2.8
97% or 3%	6.8	4.9	3.4
96% or 4%	7.8	5.6	3.9
95% or 5%	8.7	6.2	4.4
94% or 6%	9.5	6.8	4.8
92% or 8%	10.8	7.7	5.4
90% or 10%	12	8.5	6
85% or 15%	14.3	10.1	7.1
80% or 20%	16	11.4	8
75% or 25%	17.3	12.3	8.7
70% or 30%	18.3	13	9.2
65% or 35%	19.1	13.5	9.5
60% or 40%	19.6	13.9	9.8
55% or 45%	19.8	14.1	9.9
50%		20	14.2

Sampling error or standard error

This statistic provides an estimate of the true population mean i.e. the likely value we would get if we were able to measure all individuals in a population. It is based on two concepts – probability and the normal distribution. In general, we would expect in a large population very few very large values and very few very small values. Most values would tend to group around the mean (see Figure 5.1 on page 67). So, any estimate that we make is likely to be somewhere near the true population mean. Our estimates are less likely to be very much smaller or larger than the population mean. Thus, it is possible, within certain limits to estimate where the true population mean lies. The following example illustrates the point.

In a survey of vegetation characteristics in a small area, a sample of 100 observations found that 50% of the area was farmland, 14% heathland, 12% woodland and 24% other. From these figures, it is possible to state that the true population mean for woodland is somewhere around 12%. The formula for sampling error or standard error is

$\sqrt{P}$ (100-p)/n

Where P refers to the proportion of (in this case) woodland

(100-p) the proportion that is not (in this case) woodland, and

n refers to the sample size.

Thus, our estimate of the proportion of woodland that exists is

12% +/- $\sqrt{12}$ x 88/100 = 12% +/- 3.2% = from 8.8% to 15.2%.

We are therefore stating that we know that our own survey may not be totally accurate and that the true population mean is likely to lie somewhere between these limits.

The larger the sample, the more accurate the estimate. In the above example, if the proportion of woodland were still 12% but the sample size was 1,000, the standard error or sampling error would now be

12% +/- √12 x 88/1000 = 12% +/- 1.0%.

Equally, given our results from our sample of 100 we can say that

- one standard error = 12% +/- 3.2% = 8.8% – 15.2%
- two standard errors = 12% +/- 6.4% = 5.6% – 18.4%
- three standard errors = 12% +/- 9.6% = 2.4% – 21.6%.

Confidence limits

Confidence limits are based on the ideas of probability and assume the data being sampled have a normal distribution. They are usually established at the 95% and 99% levels. These levels are found by multiplying the standard error by 1.96 and 2.58 (these multipliers are in fact two and three standard deviations above and below the mean – see Figure 5.1).

Going back to the survey of vegetation, the sample mean was 12% and the standard error was 3.2%. So, at the 95% confidence level, the actual confidence level for the woodland would be

12% +/- (3.2 x 1.96) = 12% +/- 6.27 = from 18.27% to 5.63%. At the 99% confidence level, the limits would be

12% +/- (3.2 x 2.56) = 12% +/- 8.19 = from 20.19% to 3.81%.

We could express this in a slightly different way and say that if the actual woodland mean were 12%, we would expect that:

- 95% of the surveys would record the mean as lying between 5.63% and 18.27%, and
- 99% of surveys would record the mean as lying between 3.81% and 20.19%.

Data collection: some issues

In all forms of data collection, there are issues relating to safety, ethics, legality and academic rigour. Safety is a major issue – safety of those carrying out the data collection and those providing the data. A risk assessment should be made prior to the data collection period, and it should be monitored (and possibly modified) during the period of data collection.

The ethical dimension and socio-political considerations should show an awareness and concern for the attitude, emotions and beliefs of those involved in data collection/provision. You should try to minimise stress, inconvenience or harm to any participants. You should treat all participants with courtesy and respect.

Legality can refer to having permission to be in a certain area (at a certain time) and can include the photocopying of copyright materials. For academic rigour, you should try to be as accurate as possible in all of your methods of data collection, ensure a sufficient sample size, and be aware of factors that may influence your data collection.

Chapter 2

Core skills

The Edexcel specification identifies five categories of core skills which are:

● Use and annotation of illustrative and visual material.

● Use of overlays.

● Literacy.

● Numeracy.

● Questionnaire and interview techniques.

Use and annotation of illustrative and visual material

> **Annotation:** a brief sentence, descriptive and/or explanation, applied to a particular feature or features on a map, diagram or photograph.

Base maps

A **base map** at the simplest level may be only an outline of a geographical area showing just enough information to allow the reader to recognise the area concerned. Because of this, base maps are sometimes referred to as outline maps. In the past, you might have been given outline maps of the world, the UK and other countries and asked to add information to these maps. In investigative work, you are more likely to use base maps covering relatively small geographical areas such as a stretch of coastline, a section of a river valley or the central business district of an urban area.

For example, a base map of a coastal area would show the coastline and a few other features to show the limits of the map in each direction. This allows you to be clear about the extent of the geographical area covered by the base map. Then information can be added on a range of other topics such as sand dunes, surface drainage, communications and settlement. Alternatively, a base map may come from a commercial source such as Multimap. Here, more information is presented, but there is still scope for annotation. Thus, students can either draw their own base map or search the internet for the most appropriate base map for the task in hand.

Photocopied base maps or maps downloaded from the internet need careful adaptation to give them your personal 'stamp'. It is likely that you will want to insert and label a number of features on a base map. **Annotation** takes this process a significant step further by the use of short sentences to add description and maybe some very brief explanation. The objective is to produce an effective piece of geographical communication. Figure 2.1 is an example of the increasing sequence of sophistication relating to a major glacial landform. However, don't forget to include basic requirements such as a title, scale and a key.

Figure 2.1: The sequence of annotation

> **Label:** Glacial trough.
>
> **Descriptive annotation:** Glacial trough with a flat floor and steep sides.
>
> **Descriptive and explanatory annotation:** Glacial trough with a flat floor and steep sides, the result of plucking and abrasion.

In Figure 2.1 the difference between the label and the descriptive annotation is only a matter of seven short words but it adds a significant degree of information. Likewise, the difference between the latter and

the explanatory annotation is only an additional six words, but by introducing the two major processes of glacial erosion it adds an important element of explanation.

Every illustration you use should have a clear purpose. It should enhance the text and may also be of benefit in freeing up words if a word limit has been placed on the project or investigation you are carrying out. Refer clearly to your map in the text by giving it a figure number. If it is the first illustration to be used it would be 'Figure 1'. You should briefly comment on what the map shows. Base maps often provide the foundation for many or all of the other illustrations that are to follow. Base maps can be used with photographs. For example, a base map showing the course of a river might have small photographs of a waterfall and a meander.

> **Activities 2.1**
> 1. (a) Draw a base map of your school. Show the different buildings along with the different outdoor areas on the school site.
>
>   (b) Provide a label (name) for each building and outdoor area.
>
>   (c) For any four areas on the school site add an annotation to provide extra information.
>
> 2. Look at Figure 2.1. Produce another sequence of annotation beginning with the label 'upper course of a river valley'.

Sketch maps, diagrams and graphs

A **sketch map** is a summary of the main features of a more detailed map or it may just be drawn from personal observation from a good vantage point. It may in fact be a combination of both of these elements. Because it is a map there will be reference to both scale and direction. A sketch map is an example of a detailed diagram. In comparison, many diagrams are simple in nature, for example, a flow line diagram that has just three elements to it! Simplicity does not mean that a diagram lacks value. You will come across a number of simple diagrams later in this book, such as in the section on Ordnance Survey maps. The ability to draw simple diagrams which are clear and easily understood is an important core geographical skill. The same applies to **graphs**. You will come across many different types of graphs as you move through this book.

Personal observations or perceptions may form an important element of a coursework investigation or other types of geographical enquiry. As a geographer you are expected to constantly observe. Sketch maps and diagrams are a very good way of recording what you have seen and a good way to develop observation skills. Field sketches are a very important primary data collection tool. A **field sketch** is a hand-drawn summary of an environment you are looking at. In both urban and rural environments field sketching is a very useful way of recording the most important aspects of a landscape and noting the relationships between elements of such landscapes. However, it must be said that most of the field sketches that appear in books are of physical environments. The action of stopping for a period of time to sketch the landscape in front of you will often reveal details which may not have been apparent from a quicker look. This is an important way of enhancing geographical knowledge and understanding.

Figure 2.2 is an example of a good field sketch. With careful and selective annotation this sketch highlights the important geographical features of the landscape. Key features should be clearly labelled and annotated, but make sure that your sketch map is not too cluttered. This will detract from the really important details. Look for specific, small-scale features and larger more general features. The accurate use of arrows to pinpoint key features is important. A good field sketch will be viewed as a higher level technique by your fieldwork moderator.

You do not need a high level of artistic ability to produce a good field sketch. What is important is that your drawing is clear and that your annotations give good but brief description and explanation. However, if you still feel uncomfortable about drawing a field sketch, an annotated photograph is the best alternative.

The main advantage of a field sketch over a photograph is that you can omit detail that you feel is not relevant to your enquiry in a field sketch. Figure 2.3 summarises the most important aspects of a good annotated sketch map or diagram.

Figure 2.2: Example of a field sketch

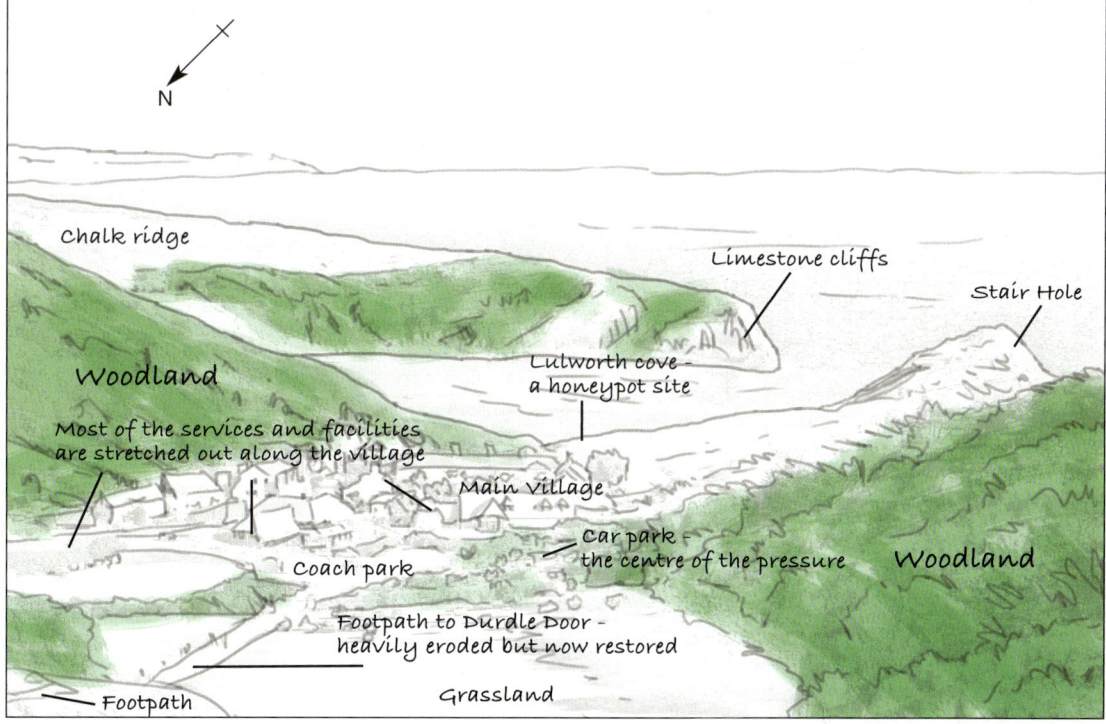

Figure 2.3: Key Points – Annotated sketch maps and diagrams

Use a pencil for your drawing so that you can make changes easily and quickly. Show clear boundaries in all directions.

Ensure that your map or diagram is large enough to show all necessary detail and can comfortably accommodate the annotations you are going to add.

Add a clear and accurate title that refers to the location of the map or diagram. Where appropriate refer to direction and scale.

Annotations should be clearly and neatly presented in short, sharp sentences which are mainly descriptive, but may also offer some brief explanation.

For a sketch diagram it might be useful to pinpoint the sketch site on a location map.

Refer clearly to your map or diagram in the text by giving it a Figure number such as 'Figure 2 is a sketch map of Lulworth Cove'.

Activities 2.2

1. What is a field sketch?

2. Find a good example of an annotated sketch map in one of your textbooks or in a book from the library. Explain why your selection is a particularly good example.

Annotated photographs

Annotated photographs should be seen as complementing field sketches rather than just an alternative to them. Like field sketches, good, fully annotated photographs are regarded as a higher level skill. Always record the precise location and the conditions of the photographs you take. This should include grid reference, the direction the photograph was taken in, weather conditions and time of day. Such information will make annotation quicker and easier in the long run as the annotation you complete in the field may be rather brief because of time limitations and you will want to elaborate on this when you get back to school.

Often photographs are taken when a field sketch is impractical because of a lack of time or other circumstances such as high winds or when the subject matter is fast-moving or short-lived such as different types of traffic movements. Attempts to capture dramatic events and unusual light conditions favour photographs over the alternatives. Photographs are also clearly preferable when group work is taking place and when field equipment is being used. It would be difficult for most people to capture these images in a field sketch. When trying to present evidence to justify conclusions you have drawn, a photograph may provide the accuracy and detail that cannot be obtained from a field sketch.

An annotated photograph shows your key perceptions about a location you have visited on fieldwork. A series of such photographs might show how:

- the type and quality of housing varies in an inner city or suburban area;
- a river and its valley change from source to mouth;
- a beach varies in profile from one end to another;
- a CBD changes from its centre to the periphery;
- a greenfield site is gradually developed.

As with sketches and diagrams, annotations should be in the form of short, sharp sentences. Moderate abbreviation is fine providing the meaning of the comment remains clear. Some annotations will be just descriptive, but where the opportunity arises some explanation should also be included. Annotation can be most effective when the photograph is placed on the page in landscape format which will allow more space for annotations on all four sides. As with field sketches, a series of annotated photographs could form a very effective part of your analysis. You should look to correlate annotated photographs with the tables and graphs showing your data analysis. Photographs are also useful to show how you carried out surveys and field measurements. They can show that you really know how to use equipment such as a flow meter or a clinometer. Figure 2.4 is an example of an annotated photograph of part of an out-of-town retail unit.

Figure 2.4: An example of an annotated photograph

Large residential area providing customer base and labour supply for the supermarket

Dual carriageway linking the rural-urban fringe with the centre of the urban area

The rural-urban fringe with farmland adjacent to urban housing

Residential suburbs comprising detached and semi-detached houses

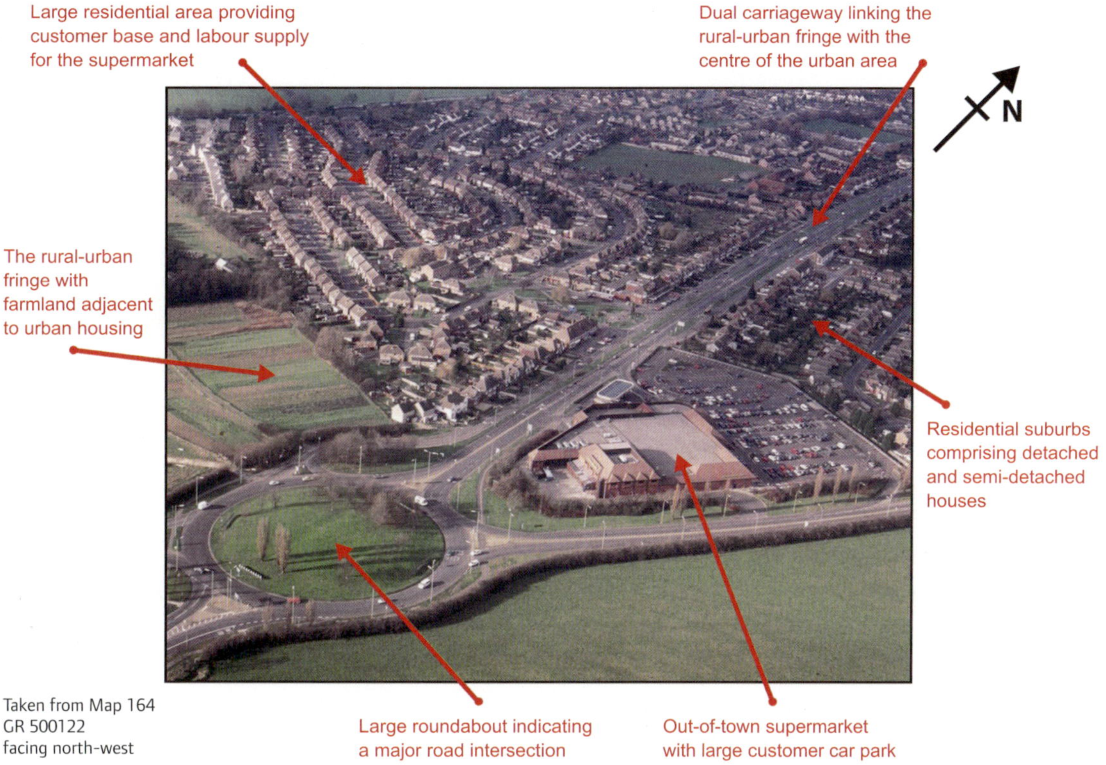

Taken from Map 164
GR 500122
facing north-west

Large roundabout indicating a major road intersection

Out-of-town supermarket with large customer car park

Geospatial, geo-located and digital imagery

Geospatial means 'of or relating to the relative position of things on the Earth's surface'. Everything you have studied in your Geography lessons at different levels should have been geospatial in nature. Geospatial data is data that has a geographic component to it – it is related to a place or places at various scales! Geospatial imagery shows the location and characteristics of both physical and human features on the surface of the Earth. Aerial photographs were the first widely used type of geospatial imagery. There have been many technological advances since the introduction of aerial photographs, satellite imagery being the most important.

Geolocation is the identification of the real-world geographic location of an object. A recent and innovative commercial example of geolocation is What3Words (Figure 2.5). What3Words has divided the Earth into 57 trillion 3m x 3m squares and given each square a unique 3 word address. This enables anyone with the What3Words app to accurately find any location in the world and share it quickly and easily with anyone else. The three words are randomly generated. For example, the Statue of Liberty is located at "planet.inches.most". The uses of What3Words include individual travel, logistics and emergency response. This system is beginning to revolutionise communication and logistics in some countries. The UN estimates that 4 billion people lack a reliable way to address their homes, with all the problems that such a situation can bring.

Digital imagery is recorded electronically to allow viewing or transmission on a computer. Such images are created through the process of digitisation. Multispectral imagery is created using technology sensitive

to particular sections of the electromagnetic spectrum. This includes sections that are beyond the range of human vision. Digital imagery may be static or continuous in nature. A number of examples appear later in this book. Digital materials include still images, videos, texts and sound recordings.

Figure 2.5: What3Words

Use of overlays

> **Overlays:** different sets of information drawn on separate clear plastic sheets that can be placed on top of each other to form a coherent map or diagram.

Overlays can be both physical and electronic. Physical overlays are constructed using a number of clear plastic sheets. A set of overlays can be viewed as a very basic geographical information system where one set of information is gradually added to another to build up a map or a diagram. It allows one layer to be drawn on a clear surface without the information contained in other layers getting in the way while the drawing of an individual sheet is taking place. For example an overlay map illustrating a fieldwork site might have individual transparent layers showing:

- Surface drainage.
- Vegetation.
- Key physical features.
- Contours.
- Settlement.
- Communications.

Layers can be presented individually or gradually added to one by one so that patterns in the physical and human landscape become apparent. Pairs of layers, for example surface drainage and settlement may illustrate particularly strong correlations. The careful construction of a key with appropriate selection of colours will be essential to the presentation of a combination of layers and particularly in the presentation of the map as a whole.

Figure 2.6: Diagram showing three overlapping layers of an overlay

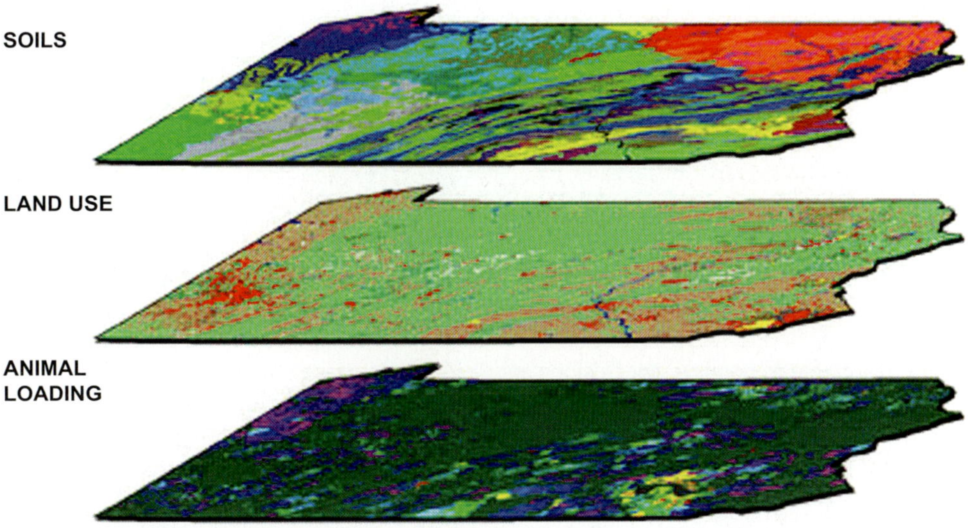

SOILS

LAND USE

ANIMAL
LOADING

Source: www.e-education.psu.edu

Following the colours used on a 1: 50,000 Ordnance Survey map can be a sensible approach both in terms of producing good contrasts and using a mix of colours that most people will be familiar with. Look at an Ordnance Survey map for the area in which you live and imagine gradually taking off different layers of information one by one. You could perhaps take off all the communications first and then the settlement, before moving on to other aspects of the map. Figure 2.6 is an example of electronic overlays.

If annotations are to be used on overlays it is important to plan their placing carefully so that the annotation on one overlay does not obscure the annotation on another. Ensure that in total there are not too many annotations.

Activities 2.3
1. What is an overlay?
2. What are the advantages of this geographical technique?

Literacy

Literacy: the ability to identify, understand, interpret, create, communicate and compute, using printed and written materials associated with varying contexts (The United Nations Educational, Scientific and Cultural Organisation – UNESCO).

Literacy involves a range of skills relating to language as the UNESCO definition above shows. As you have developed literacy skills in general and geographical literacy skills in particular you will gradually have developed greater ability to describe, explain, hypothesise and apply your best reading, writing and thinking skills to the places and issues you have come across in geography.

The terms geographical literacy and geographical fluency are often used to describe the ability to produce good quality written analyses in this subject. Clarity of expression is the most important aspect of any geographical investigation or presentation. This means saying what you want to say in as clear a way as possible, leaving no room for ambiguity. While it would be possible (although unusual and limiting) to produce a geographical investigation without using any illustrations, it would not be possible to do the reverse and to have no text, relying only on illustrations. Thus, the text is the essential part of any geography project or enquiry which should be enhanced significantly by the addition of illustrations.

Literacy skills in geography include:

- using geographical terms correctly;
- expressing ideas and hypotheses tentatively;
- describing and comparing effectively;
- structuring explanations clearly;
- introducing and engaging in debate in an incisive and interesting way;
- showing understanding of different values and attitudes; and
- being able to come to conclusions and to evaluate.

Geographic literacy involves drawing on an increasingly wide range of geographical factors in framing ideas using drafting and editing skills. This involves reading and understanding material from a range of different sources. Some of these sources may present conflicting views on a topic so the ability to check for bias is important. For example, think of the current debate regarding climate change.

Geography, like any subject discipline, has a very specific language. A good piece of geographical work will use the particular forms of language and literacy best suited to posing and answering geographical questions. Getting used to using a geographical dictionary is an important step in developing literacy skills in the subject.

Some sources of information may present conflicting views on a topic so the ability to check for bias is important.

Geographic information processing skills can be grouped under five headings:

- asking geographic questions;
- acquiring geographic information;
- presenting geographic information;
- interpreting geographic information;
- developing and testing geographic information.

Quality of written communication

The overall quality of your written communication is important in both examinations and in all the assignments you produce throughout the course. In the examination the specification states that candidates must:

- Ensure the text is legible and that spelling, punctuation and grammar are accurate so that meaning is clear.
- Select and use a form and style of writing appropriate to purpose and to complex subject matter.
- Organise information clearly and coherently, using specialist vocabulary when appropriate.

The mark scheme for examination papers includes an overall assessment of the quality of written communication by embedding the three strands above within the levels of marking criteria.

Developing literacy skills for geographical writing

There are a number of strategies for improving your ability to complete essays and other written tasks in geography. For all essay questions and other written tasks you need to

- examine closely the wording of the question, and
- plan your answer.

Read the question carefully and underline the command words and the topic to be discussed. Command words tell you what to do in the essay or how to use the material. There are a number of such command words including:

- *analyse*   examine carefully the details of a theory, pattern, distribution
- *assess*   estimate the importance of
- *compare*   look for similarities and differences between features
- *contrast*   bring out the differences
- *criticise*   give a critical account of (discuss rather than blame)
- *describe*   show the details and characteristics of
- *discuss*   examine by argument giving the pros and cons
- *distinguish*   show the differences between
- *evaluate*   show the relative importance
- *examine*   investigate in detail
- *explain*   show in detail how something works
- *illustrate*   show with the use of case studies and examples
- *justify*   present an argument for
- *outline*   show the general principles or main features rather than minute details

There are three main requirements in most essays – description, explanation and evaluation. **Description** requires factual recall, for example describing the characteristics of central business districts or tropical rain forests. In contrast, **explanation** requires you to give reasons and account for why a particular place or geographical situation is the way it is. **Evaluation** requires you to give an opinion based on the evidence you have presented throughout the essay.

It is vital to think about the essay and to plan it. Quality is more important than length. One way of planning an essay is known as the points-group-order method. Write down a list of points that are relevant to the essay and then group them, and finally put them into order of importance. Mind maps are an alternative strategy that many students mind useful.

A good essay usually has three clear sections – introduction, body and conclusion. Writing the introduction is a key skill. Most examiners have a good idea of the grade a candidate will achieve after they have read the introduction! The introduction should:

- define the terms used in the title.
- show the line of argument that will be taken.
- list the factors that are important.
- state which examples and case studies will be used.

The introduction needs to be clear and full of impact rather like the introduction in a newspaper article which catches your attention, shows the main line of argument, and has you wanting for more.

The main body of the essay develops the arguments. Each paragraph should have a key sentence or key point and the rest of the paragraph explains and provides evidence. Paragraphs must be linked, and this is done in a variety of ways:

- referring back to the point above (the result of this is to cause…).
- linking in a time-sequence (next, after etc.).
- comparisons (there are also environmental problems in shanty towns).
- contrasts (by contrast, the UK's economy is based on services).

Throughout the essay the quality of language needs to be high. Thus, it is important to use key words and phrases that make the essay read well, as well as allowing it to flow. These words and phrases are small but have a major impact on how clearly the arguments come across.

The conclusion is more than just a summary. It may

- assess the changing nature of the topic.
- examine the changing importance of factors involved.
- draw out the uniqueness of the material used (every example is different).
- look at the contrasts between developed countries and developing countries.
- look to the future (how will the subject change in the next 25 years).
- end with a question, for example 'Even if we can predict earthquakes and volcanoes can we stop people from living in hazardous areas?'.

Reliability of sources of information

You will be aware from reading different newspapers and watching a range of TV channels that an 'issue' or 'event' can be presented in different ways. For example, many people are influenced by the opinions of prominent journalists such as George Monbiot (*The Guardian*) and Christopher Booker (*Daily Mail*). The former has for long warned about human-induced global warming and the need to take very decisive international action. The latter holds very different opinions, branding the whole issue as a gigantic hoax based on very flawed scientific evidence and also a very costly mistake because of the ill-conceived measures employed to try to reduce the 'problem'. Booker argues that constructing wind farms in particular is a massive waste of money. Both journalists write with conviction and skill so how do you decide who is right?

It is important when researching an issue, particularly one that is generally viewed as controversial, that you look at a variety of different sources of information. Where there is a range of opinion, make a note of it and try to understand why writers have developed different opinions about an issue or topic. It may be the case that you have to go back to original source material such as a United Nations report rather than rely on a brief newspaper or television synopsis of that report. Selective reporting can sometimes lose the emphasis and direction of an original text.

As your literacy skills become more sophisticated you will learn to recognise the difference between an objective view of an event and a biased account. Learning to identify textual bias is part of becoming media literate. However, it is not just what is written, but also what may be omitted. The media in most countries tend to focus very heavily on their 'home' country and other countries which they think their readers are most interested in hearing about. Why is it that a natural disaster in one part of the world receives a very high level of media attention whereas a natural disaster of equal severity in another country attracts far less media attention? Such a situation has sometimes been referred to as 'high-attention crisis versus low-attention crisis'.

A number of prominent writers have increasingly referred to the present time as the 'Post-Truth Era'. This refers to a situation where the previous distinction between truth and lies has become blurred with the increasingly frequent use of ambiguous statements that are not exactly the truth but fall just short of a lie! In 2016, "post-truth" was selected as the Oxford Dictionaries' Word of the Year because of its widespread use in terms of the conduct and media coverage of the Brexit referendum and the US presidential election.

Never before has so much information been available, but much of it is of low quality and a certain amount is deliberately deceptive! If in any doubt always try to check with sources of information that have a good reputation for reliability.

Coding techniques

Coding can be a useful skill to develop when analysing text. The core idea of coding is that a body of text is indexed to make it easier to analyse and recognise patterns and trends. The process involves searching the text for similar themes, concepts and key words and marking the relevant areas of the text with a code colour.

A simple example would be to use colour highlighters on a body of text. You could, for example, highlight all the facts presented in a piece of text in blue and all attempts to interpret the facts in red. Along the same lines, if you were reading an article about the North American Free Trade Area (NAFTA) you could use three different colours to highlight references to the three member countries, the USA, Canada and Mexico. This would facilitate grouping all references to each country together in a systematic manner. Of course, a much larger number of colours could be used to analyse a complex body of text. The number of codes (colours in this case) can be increased as new themes etc appear in the text. Coding can help to illustrate the links between themes, concepts and key words. It is a skill that may take some time when first attempted, but you will soon quicken your pace of work the more times you apply this skill.

Numeracy

Numeracy is the ability to interpret and use numbers. It involves developing the confidence and ability to judge the best mathematical technique to use in a particular situation. Geography is a numerate subject, using mathematical concepts in a wide variety of ways. You will have developed and used numeracy skills in your study of Geography on many occasions. For example, numeracy skills are fundamental to the understanding of Ordnance Survey maps. The most obvious examples relate to scale, grid references, the interpretation of contour patterns and measurements of distances between places.

Think of the number of tables and graphs in your textbook you would not be able to understand without the numerical ability you have developed over time. Also think how such tables and graphs have become more complex as you have moved from Key Stage 3, through GCSE to A-Level. If you move on to study Geography at university, the level of numeracy required will become even more challenging.

Look at one case study in your textbook. How many references to numeracy does it contain? Describe them and rank them in degree of difficulty. Slowly flick through this book. Which aspects of numeracy stand out? Which do you think you already understand and which are clearly more difficult?

Measurement involves giving a numerical value to the amount or quantity of a phenomenon according to certain rules. This allows everyone to understand what the measurement means. It is generally accepted that there are four different scales of measurement. These are as follows:

Nominal scale – classifying a phenomenon into types, for example a rock type such as shale.

Ordinal scale – the ranking of data.

Interval scale – the ranking of data with equality of intervals between the classes.

Ratio scale – the critical point here is the need for equality of ratios. This is achieved by having equality of intervals and a real zero point.

> ### Activities 2.4
> 1. (a) What is coding?
>
>   (b) Give a simple example of the use of coding.
>
> 2. List the four different scales of measurement.

Questionnaire and interview techniques

The **questionnaire** is a very useful technique to investigate patterns, trends and attitudes. It is often used to complement information obtained by other techniques such as observation. Questionnaire surveys involve both setting questions and obtaining answers. The questions are pre-planned and set out on a specially prepared form.

> **Questionnaires** are documents that ask the same questions of all individuals in the sample.

The questionnaire survey is probably the most widely used method to obtain primary data in human geography. In the wider world questionnaires are used for a variety of purposes, including market research by manufacturing and retail companies, and to test public opinion prior to political elections. Questionnaires may contain both:

- Closed questions with a fixed choice of answers to generate data for easy analysis.
- Open questions with space to give any answer for more detailed individual answers.

One of the most important decisions you have to make is how many questionnaires you are going to complete. The general rules to follow here are similar to those for sampling, set out in the previous chapter. Remember, if you have too few questionnaire results, you will not be able to draw valid conclusions. For most types of study, 25 questionnaires is probably the minimum you would need to draw reasonable conclusions. On the other hand it is unlikely you would have time for more than 100 unless you were collecting data as part of a group.

A good questionnaire:

- Has a limited number of questions that take no more than a few minutes to answer;
- Is clearly set out so that the questioner can move quickly from one question to the next – people do not like to be kept waiting; the careful use of tick boxes can help this objective:
- Is carefully worded so that the respondents are clear about the meaning of each question;
- Follows a logical sequence so that respondents can see 'where the questionnaire is going' – if a questionnaire is too complicated and long-winded people may decide to stop halfway through;
- Avoids questions that are too personal;
- Begins with the quickest questions to answer and leaves the longer/more difficult questions to the end; and,
- Reminds the questioner to thank respondents for their cooperation.

The disadvantages of questionnaires are:

- The response rate may be lower than you anticipate. Many people may not want to cooperate for a variety of reasons. Some people will simply be too busy, others may be uneasy about talking to strangers, while some people may be concerned about the possibility of identity theft.
- Research has indicated that people do not always provide accurate answers in surveys. Some people are tempted to give the answer that they think the questioner wants to hear or the answer they think shows them in the best light.
- Questionnaires are not suitable to investigate long, complex issues.

As with other forms of data collection, it is advisable to carry out a brief pilot survey first. It could be that some words or questions you find easy to understand cause problems for some people. Amending the questionnaire in the light of the pilot survey before you begin the survey proper will make everything go much more smoothly. Figure 2.7 shows the difference between a good, carefully constructed questionnaire and a much less effective one prepared in haste.

Delivering the questionnaire

There are really three options:

- Approach people in the street or in another public place.

- Knock on people's doors.

- Post questionnaires to people. With this approach you could either collect the questionnaire later or enclose a stamped addressed envelope. The latter method is costly and experience shows that response rates are rarely above 30 per cent. Another disadvantage is that you will be unable to ask for clarification if some responses are unclear.

A survey of shopping habits may produce considerable differences between male and female respondents and between different age groups. In this case you could use a stratified sample divided by gender and the percentage of population in each age group.

The time of day may also be important in delivering a questionnaire. In the example given above, very few people in some age groups may be around at a certain time of day. For example, most teenagers will be in school or college at mid-morning on a weekday.

Figure 2.7: Two questionnaires – one good and one bad

A good questionnaire

Introduction: "Excuse me, I am doing a school geography project. Could I ask you one or two quick questions about where you go shopping?"

1. How often do you come shopping in this town centre?
   More than once a week ☐
   Weekly ☐   Occasionally ☐

2. How do you travel here?
   Walk ☐   Car ☐   Bus ☐   Train/Tube ☐
   Other ....

3. Roughly where do you live?
   ....

4. Why do you come here rather than any other shopping centre?
   Near to home ☐   Near to work ☐
   More choice ☐   Pleasant environment ☐
   Other ....

5. What sort of things do you normally buy here?
   Groceries ☐   Clothes/shoes ☐
   Everything ☐
   Other ....

6. Do you shop anywhere else, and if so where?
   ....

7. Why do you go shopping there?
   ....

8. What do you buy there?
   ....

9. Sex: M ☐   F ☐   Age: (estimate) under 20 ☐
                        20-30 ☐   30-60 ☐   Over 60 ☐

"Thank you very much for your help."

A bad questionnaire

Introduction: "Excuse me, but I wonder if I could ask you some questions?"

1. Where do you live?
   ....

2. How do you get here?
   ....

3. Do you come shopping here often?
   ....

4. Why do you come here?
   ....

5. Do you buy high- or low-order goods here?
   ....

6. Is this a good shopping centre and if so, why?
   ....

7. Where else you do you shopping?
   ....

8. Do you shop there because it is cheaper or nearer to your home?
   ....

9. How old are you?
   ....

"Right, that's it then."

Source: Cambridge IGCSE Geography, P. Guinness & G. Nagle, 2014, Hodder Education, Fig. 5, p. 270

Interviews

Interviews are more detailed interactions than questionnaires. They will generally involve talking to a relatively small number of people. For example, a study of an industrial estate might involve interviews with the directors of six different companies if you were trying to find out why companies chose to locate

Interviews enable you to ask open-ended questions that create more in-depth data sets than those afforded by questionnaires.

on the estate. An interview is much more of a discussion than a questionnaire, although you should still have a pre-planned question sheet. Interviews enable you to ask open-ended questions that create more in-depth data sets than those afforded by questionnaires. Interviews are thus more likely to produce unexpected responses than questionnaires.

A good interview will be based on preparatory stages similar to those for a questionnaire. As the number of people interviewed will be relatively small, it is even more important to be able to justify your choice of sample. If you are investigating a controversial issue where there are three obvious interest groups, you will need to ensure that your interviews give equal coverage to each group. It can be a good idea to record interviews, but you should ask the interviewee's permission first. It might be the case that a potential respondent may not be able to offer a face-to-face interview, but is instead willing to offer the opportunity of a telephone interview. This should not present a problem, although it will be important to state that this was a telephone interview in your analysis and to note any limitations that this mode of communication created compared to your face-to-face interviews.

At the postgraduate level of geographical enquiry, researchers may embed themselves in ethnic communities in different countries for a period of weeks or months with regular interviews/discussion with individual members and groups within the community along with continuous observation. Such research is called ethnographic analysis. This form of research has proved to be particularly illuminating in the study of migration, for example, in the understanding of gender differences in migration.

An **interview** consists of a series of pre-planned oral questions by the interviewer and oral responses by the research participant.

Activities 2.5

1. Give three characteristics of a good questionnaire.

2. What is the difference between closed questions and open questions?

3. State three ways in which interviews are likely to be different to questionnaires.

Ordnance Survey maps

Scale and grid references

As with atlas maps, Ordnance Survey maps come at a variety of scales. The smallest scale maps published by the Ordnance Survey are at a scale of 1: 1,000,000 while the largest scale OS maps are at 1: 1,250. Larger scale maps show more detail than smaller scale maps. Figure 2.8 is a summary of the various scales of map published by the Ordnance Survey. The OS maps used by geographers are mainly at the scales of 1: 50,000 and 1: 25,000.

Figure 2.8: Scales and uses of Ordnance Survey maps

Scale	1 cm =	Use
1: 1,000,000	10 km	This is the scale of OS map to see the whole of Great Britain at a glance.
1: 625,000	6.25 km	For administrative purposes by businesses and government departments wanting to view very large areas of the country. Also useful for planning journeys over long distances.
1: 250,000	2.5 km	These maps are used for planning routes or navigation.
1: 50,000	500 m	General-purpose use, for example, business planning, motoring, walking and cycling.
1: 25,000	250 m	Used by walkers and other outdoor enthusiasts but they also contain enough detail for local area planning purposes.
1: 10,000	100 m	Most useful for town planners, builders and farmers who require a high level of detail for a relatively large area.
1: 2500	25 m	Mapping at 1: 1,250 and 1: 2500 scales is used by central and local government, utilities (gas, electricity, water and telecommunications companies) and other organisations wanting highly detailed mapping for planning or business management purposes. Most rural areas are covered at 1: 2,500 scale.
1: 1250	12.5 m	This scale of mapping covers urban areas only with similar usage as the 1: 2,500 maps covering rural areas.

Grid references

Grid lines are drawn on large and medium scale maps so that a place can be located precisely from the grid reference. There are two sets of grid lines:

● **Eastings** are the vertical grid lines on maps. They increase in value from west to east (left to right). This is why they are called eastings. On Figure 2.9 the vertical grid lines 63-68 are eastings.

● **Northings** are the horizontal grid lines. They increase in value from south to north (bottom to top). This is why they are called northings. On Figure 2.9 the horizontal grid lines 12-17 are northings.

A **four figure grid reference** is used to locate a grid square. The first two digits refer to the easting value and the second two digits to the northing value. Unless the location this gives is at the edge of the map it will be at the intersection of four grid squares. The square in question will be the one to the north east (upper right). Figure 2.9 gives two examples.

Figure 2.9: Finding 4-figure grid references

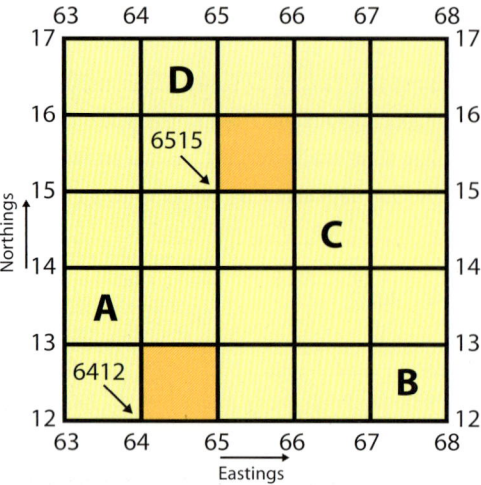

A six figure grid reference is needed to locate an exact point within a grid square. Once you have found the correct grid square, use the third figure (the final easting number) and the sixth figure (the final northing number) to find the precise location (Figure 2.10). This is usually done visually but a ruler can be used to be more precise. Two examples are given on Figure 2.10 to show how this works.

Figure 2.10: Finding 6-figure grid references

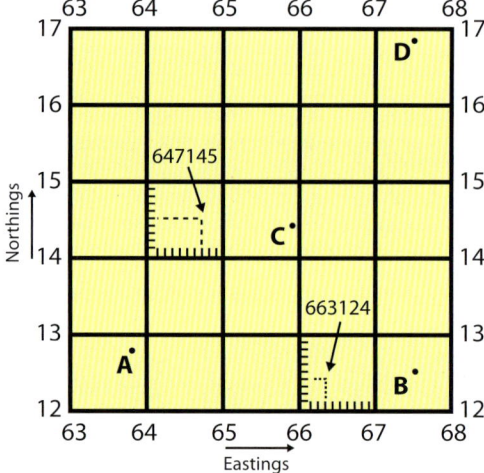

Activities 2.6

1. What are (a) northings; (b) eastings?

2. Look at Figure 2.9. Give the four-figure grid references for the squares marked A, B, C and D.

3. Look at Figure 2.10. Give the six-figure grid references for the points marked A, B, C and D.

Methods of showing relief on maps

Relief: the height and shape of the land together form relief.

Contour line: a line on a map joining places of equal height above sea level.

Contour interval: the difference in height between each contour on a map.

The height and shape of the land together form relief. Relief is important because it has a major effect on human geography and other aspects of physical geography. Relief can be illustrated in a number of ways:

- Ancient mapmakers used pictures or physiographic diagrams to depict really significant features. However, this technique is rarely used today because these diagrams are not drawn to scale and therefore lack accuracy.

- Layer-colouring is a technique frequently used for atlas maps. The lowest layer of land, usually below 100m is generally coloured mid-green. The next layer, 100-250m is light green. This is usually followed by layers of yellow, light brown, dark brown and purple. In very high landscapes some areas may be left white to indicate snow covered summits. The sequence of colour can change from atlas to atlas along with the altitudinal range of each colour. This technique is visually impressive which is why it is used for so many atlas maps. However, there are some criticisms of this technique: (a) Such maps show abrupt rather than gradual changes, (b) the dark shading for very high land can partially obscure other detail, (c) some colours may convey a different perception to the one desired in the minds of some readers.

- Hachures are short lines drawn at right angles to contours to give an indication of gradient. The closer the lines, the steeper the slope, although this is not quantified. This technique was used more frequently by early map-makers than it is today as it is mainly a visual rather than a detailed and accurate method.

- Hill shading/oblique illumination shows significant features from an imaginary source of light. The light source is usually assumed to be in the north-west corner of the map. The result of this is that slopes in the south and east, which are under shadow, are more darkly shaded than those in the north and west. This is another technique much favoured by early map-makers.

- Contour lines, spot heights, triangulation pillars and bench marks are the most important methods used on modern large- and medium-scale maps. As such, these methods will be discussed in more detail below.

Contour lines

The height of the land is its altitude above mean sea level. It is stated in metres. The main method of representing relief is by the use of **contour lines**. A contour line is a line on a map linking places of the same height above mean sea level. So, if you find a contour line labelled 50 metres and follow it as far as it goes on a map, every place along the line will be at an altitude of 50 metres above mean sea level. Figure 2.11 is an example of a contour pattern on a map. Here the distance between each contour is 20 metres. This is known as the contour interval. The contour interval may differ according to the scale of the map.

Figure 2.11: Diagram illustrating the relationship between contour lines and relief

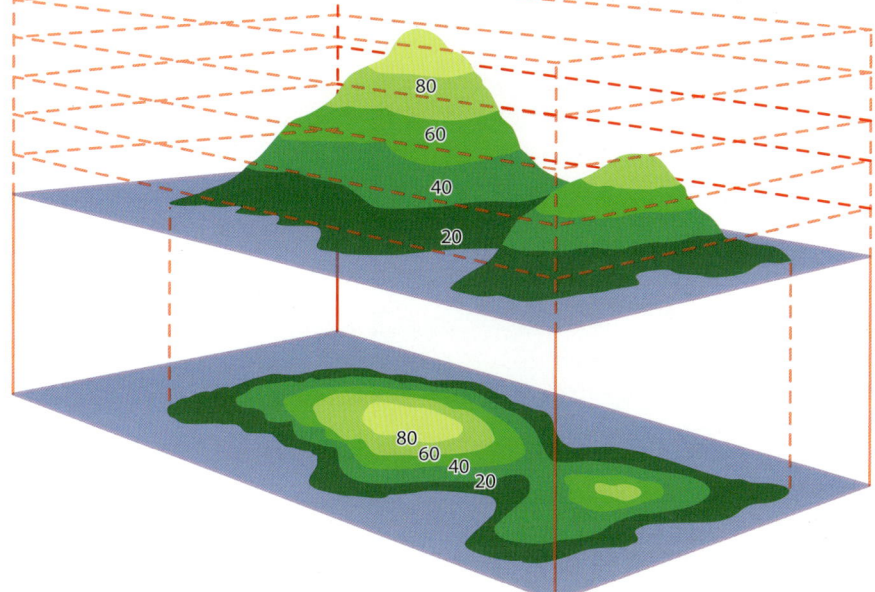

Figure 2.11 shows the relationship between a contour pattern (shown at the bottom of the diagram) and the relief it depicts (shown at the top of the diagram). Notice how the contours decrease in area as the land becomes higher. This is because the distance around the top of the hill is considerably less than around the bottom of the hill. A contour line is an example of an isoline. An isoline joins something of equal value. Different types of isolines will be discussed later in this chapter.

Not all the contours on a map have a number written on them because this would produce too much clutter on the map. However, if a contour has not been given a height figure, you can work it out using those contours which have been allocated a height figure. The cartographers who drew the map will have made sure that this is the case. Only if a point lies exactly on a contour line can its height above sea level be given precisely. So, if a farm lies somewhere between the 20 and 40 metre contours, and you were asked to describe the altitude of the farm, you would need to mention both contours in your answer.

On a real Ordnance Survey map the contour pattern can sometimes become very complex if the relief of the landscape changes often and steeply. To make the contour pattern easier to read, **major contours**, are drawn slightly thicker than the other contours. Major contours are depicted at 50 metre intervals on 1: 50,000 OS maps. Thus, in very steep landscapes, look at the major contours first to gain an overall impression of the general shape of the landscape. Once you have done this you can study the remaining contours to gain more detail. It is useful to remember that when reading contour lines on a map the numbering on them reads uphill. If you are unsure whether the land is rising or falling, this will be a help.

Spot heights, triangulation pillars and bench marks

Additional information about relief is shown by the use of **spot heights**. This gives the height above sea level of an exact position. A spot height is a dot printed on the map with its height in metres written alongside. Spot heights often mark the lowest and highest points in a landscape and are often given along roads. Heights may also be shown alongside the sign for a **triangulation pillar**. On an OS map this is a small blue triangle with a dot in the middle. In the landscape it is a concrete or stone pillar. The top of the pillar contains grooves in which surveyors set their instruments. Triangulation points are the most accurately surveyed points in the landscape.

Bench marks give exact heights along roads and railways. These heights are marked on stones, bricks or bronze plates on walls of buildings and other convenient places.

Photo 2.1: A triangulation pillar in NW England

Understanding the shape of the land by looking at a map is a very useful skill. It can be essential if you are going to walk in hilly or mountainous terrain. Use all the information on the map to help you. The contour lines, spot heights and triangulation pillars should set the basic scene for you while the identification of basic landforms covered in the next few paragraphs will also help. The positioning of human geography features such as settlements and lines of communication will provide useful added evidence.

Figure 2.12: 1: 50,000 map extract of the Isle of Anglesey

Source: Ordnance Survey

Activities 2.7

1. Study Figure 2.11. Why is the 20 metre contour line much more extensive than the 60 metre contour line?

2. What is meant by the contour interval?

3. Why are some contour lines drawn thicker than others on OS maps?

4. What methods are used to provide additional information about relief?

5. Look at the OS map extract, Figure 2.12:

   (a) What is the grid reference of the lighthouse at the end of Holyhead's harbour wall?

   (b) What is the map evidence that tourism is important in the area?

   (c) What is the evidence that an ancient settlement existed at Holyhead?

   (d) What is the approximate distance of the dual carriageway shown on the map?

Valleys and spurs

The patterns made by contour lines on a map help us to identify distinctive features of relief known as landforms. **Valleys** and **spurs** are the most common landscape features found in an area where the altitude varies. Both features can be easily recognised by the contour patterns they form.

> **Valley:** a depression in the landscape eroded by a river or a glacier. It is usually the lowest point in the local landscape.
>
> **Spur:** a finger of higher land projecting out into a valley.

Look at Figure 2.13 which shows a landscape of valleys and spurs. The top diagram shows the contour pattern, while the bottom diagram shows the landscape in cross section. Notice that for a spur the contours form a 'U' or 'V' shape, with the head of the 'U' or 'V' pointing down slope. The contour pattern for the valleys also forms a 'U' or 'V' shape, but here the head of the shape points upslope. Figure 2.13 shows three spurs with two intervening valleys. Most, but not all valleys contain rivers or streams which are shown by a thin blue line on an Ordnance Survey map. The presence of a river helps to confirm the identification of a valley.

Figure 2.13: Contour diagram and cross section showing valleys and spurs

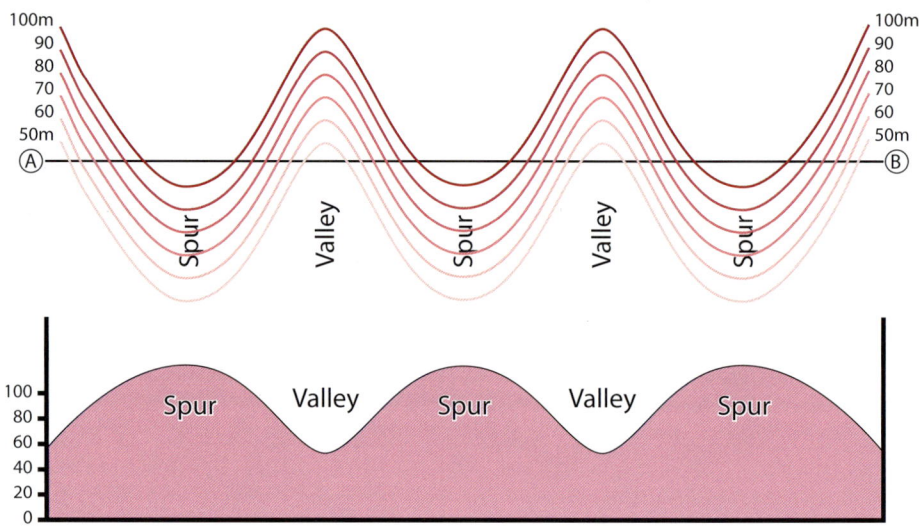

Slopes

> **Slope:** a slanting area of the landscape.

A slope occurs in the landscape when the land is not completely flat. Some slopes are steep while others are gentle. **Slopes** are found on the sides of valleys and spurs. On some slopes the angle of slope remains the same – the slope is said to be constant. On other slopes the angle of slope may change. A clinometer is an instrument that can be used to measure the angle of a slope. There are many slopes shown in Figure 2.13 and they are all quite steep. Contour lines and the pattern they make tell us a lot about slopes. When contour lines are spaced far apart the land is quite flat. When the contour lines are very close together the land is very steep. When the land is too steep for contour lines a symbol for a cliff is used. The main types of slope are:

- Concave slopes: the gradient is steep at the top of the slope, but decreases towards the bottom. Thus, the contour lines are close together at the top, and then become further apart towards the bottom.

- Convex slopes: here the gradient is steep at the bottom of the slope, but becomes more gentle towards the top. Thus, the contour lines are close together at the bottom, becoming more widely spaced at the top.

- Uniform or 'even' slopes: this is where the gradient is the same throughout the slope or changes very little. The result on a map is that the contour lines are evenly spaced.

- Stepped or terraced slopes: Some slopes are made up of alternating gentle and steep sections. In the gentle sections the contours are widely spaced. In the steep sections the contours are much closer together.

Figure 2.14 shows these four types of slope in cross section and how they look on a contour map.

Figure 2.14

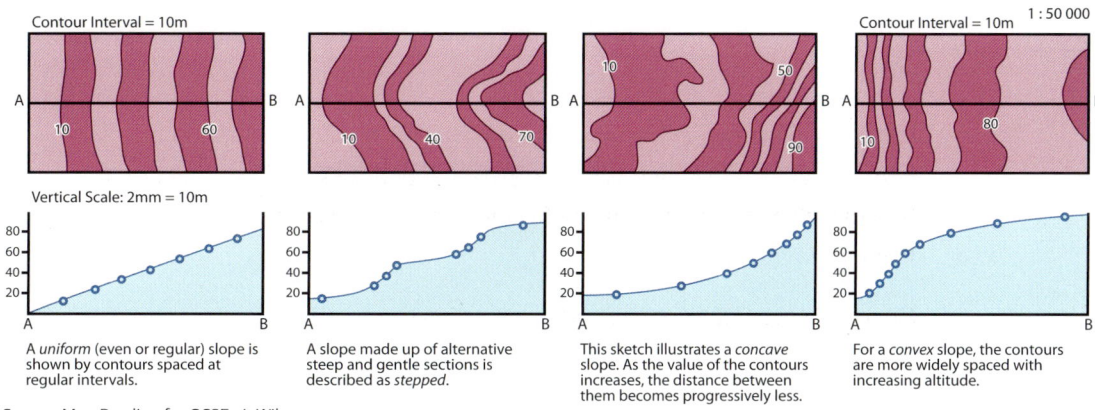

Source: Map Reading for GCSE, J. Wilson

Another relatively common landscape feature is an escarpment which has two contrasting slopes. On one side is the steep scarp slope (Figure 2.15), and on the other side the more gentle dip slope. The contour lines indicating the scarp slope are closely packed, but more widely spaced apart on the dip slope. The dip slope is usually dissected by valleys and spurs.

Figure 2.15: An escarpment

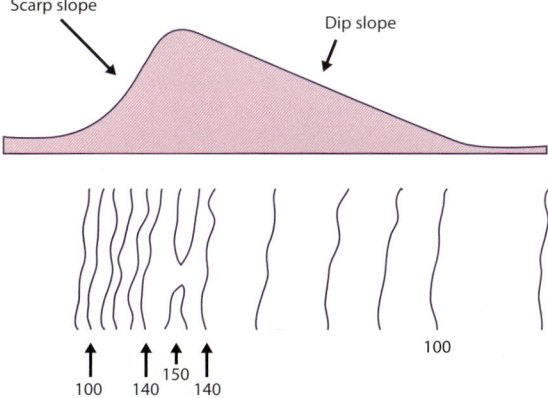

Gradient

> **Gradient:** the degree to which a slope inclines.

The gradient of a slope is its steepness. We can get a rough idea of the gradient of a slope by looking at the contour pattern. If the contour lines are close together the slope is steep, and if they are far apart the land is relatively flat. However, these are not very accurate descriptions. To measure gradient accurately two measurements are required:

- The vertical distance between two points. This can be calculated using contour lines or spot heights.

- The horizontal distance between the two places. This may not be a straight line. For example, a meandering stream would not be straight.

The gradient of a slope can be expressed in three ways:

- Ratio: It is important to use the same units for both vertical and horizontal measurements. Divide the difference in horizontal distance (D) by the height (H). If the answer is, for example, '10' express it as '1:10' ('one in ten') or '5' as '1 in 5' ('one in five'). This means that for every 10 metres along you rise 1 metre, or for every 5 metres in length the land rises (or drops) 1 metre.

- Percent: Alternatively, divide the height (H) by the difference in horizontal distance (D) and multiply by 100% (H/D x 100%). This expresses the gradient as a percentage. For example, a road with a gradient of 10% rises one metre for every 10 metres of horizontal length.

As few slopes are perfectly uniform, it is more accurate to refer to the average gradient when calculations are made.

Photo 2.2: Road sign indicating the gradient of the road

Activities 2.8

1. What is a spur?

2. Which physical feature can help to confirm the presence of a valley?

3. Which instrument can be used to measure the angle of a slope?

4. Describe the four types of slope illustrated in Figure 2.14.

5. (a) Describe the features of an escarpment.

   (b) On a copy of the contour diagram in Figure 2.15, add the heights of the contour lines which are not labelled.

6. (a) Define the term gradient.

   (b) Explain how the gradient of a slope can be expressed as a ratio.

Sketch maps drawn from OS maps

Sketch map: a map drawn from observation rather than from exact measurement, representing the main features of an area.

The use of base maps and sketch maps has already been considered from the point of view of annotation. Here the emphasis is on construction. A sketch map is a simplified illustration of an area which shows the basic positions of certain features of particular interest to the observer. Figure 2.16 is an example of a sketch map of Studland on the Isle of Purbeck, Dorset. This sketch map was compiled in the following way:

- The information shown on the sketch map was taken from (a) the 1: 50,000 Ordnance Survey map of the area and (b) personal field observation when an A-Level group were taken on a walk along Studland beach and through the sand dunes.

- A clear border was drawn on the paper leaving sufficient room for annotations on all sides. It is important that the area available for drawing fits the general shape of the region to be illustrated.

- The coastline and other main outline features were added.

- The 10 metre contour was inserted so that slightly higher areas of this generally low-lying region could be identified and it was clear that the land on the seaward side of the sketch map was below 10 metres in altitude.

- Other features were drawn in such as the sand dunes, Little Sea and areas of marsh.

- Key labels such as Studland Bay, South Haven Point and Poole Harbour were inserted as important points in themselves but also so that the limits of the sketch map were clear to see.

- Annotations were then added. The detail of the annotations was clearly related to the focus of the investigation.

- Finally the sketch map was given a full title, a scale, a key, and a North-point.

Figure 2.16: A sketch map of Studland beach and dunes

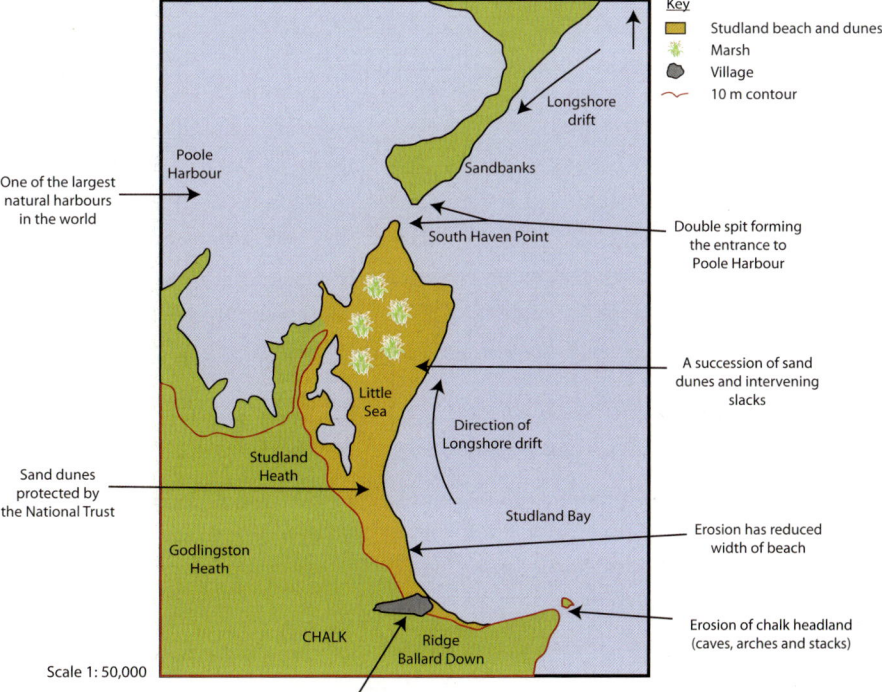

The sketch map provided the illustrative foundation for an investigation and as such is arguably the most important illustration in the study. It was allocated a Figure number and referred to as such in the text. It provided the basis for a number of other illustrations including cross-sections and photographs and reference was made to these links where appropriate.

Chapter 3

Cartographic skills

Photo 3.1: Small group of students looking at a map

> **Cartography:** the study and practice of compiling or drawing maps or charts.

Cartographic skills are an essential element of the geographers 'toolbox'. Arguably the most basic geographical skill is the ability to use an atlas; to understand what each map is showing and to have a clear idea of scale, direction and position on the Earth's surface. We can transfer these skills to maps at a larger scale, particularly Ordnance Survey maps. The detail may be shown in a different way but the fundamental principles are the same. If you look at a standard school atlas you will see that maps can be presented in a variety of different ways such as the use of dots, shading and isolines to convey regional differences. It is important to understand such techniques if you are to make full use of atlases, Ordnance Survey maps, textbooks and other geographical materials. You may also want to use such skills in producing your own geographical analyses. Thus, cartographic skills fall into two parts:

- the ability to understand different types of maps and diagrams relating to maps, and
- the ability to construct such maps and diagrams to a reasonable standard.

The cartographic skills identified by the Edexcel specification are as follows:

- Atlas maps.
- Maps with located proportional symbols.
- Maps showing movement.
- Maps showing spatial patterns.

Maps form the basis of cartography. A map is a simplified representation or model of reality in which different symbols are used to represent features in the real world. Maps are sophisticated information sources. The human eye can interpret a wide variety of information from a map just from the pictorial content.

Atlas maps

Scale

Atlas maps come at a variety of scales. For example:

- A double page map of southern Britain may be shown at a scale of 1: 1,200,000 with 1 cm representing 12 km.

- A full page map of the UK may be at a scale of 1: 4,000,000. Here 1 cm would be equivalent to 40 km.

- A map of Europe spread over two pages might be at a scale of 1: 16,000,000 with 1 cm representing 160 km.

- A map of the entire world set over a double page could be at a scale of 1: 77,500,000 so that 1 cm equals 775 km.

These examples were all taken from one standard school atlas. The scale of an atlas map is generally shown in the lower left hand or right hand corner of the page, but this can vary. It is customary for the scale to be given numerically and in a linear format.

Figure 3.1: Atlas map of Wales

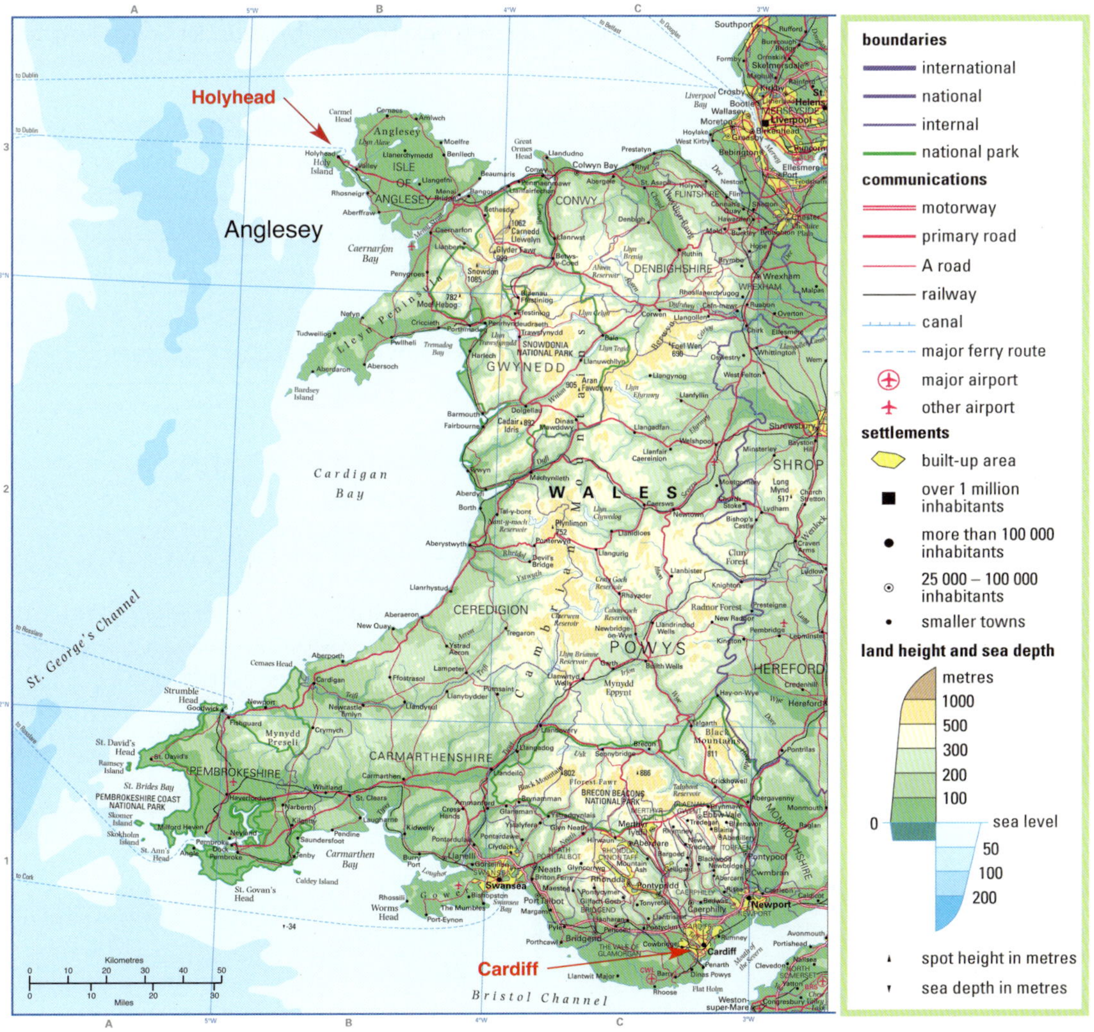

Source: Oxford Student Atlas, OUP

Figure 3.1 is an atlas map of Wales. An Ordnance Survey map extract of part of this region, focussing on the ferry port of Holyhead, at a scale of 1: 50,000 was shown on page 22 (Figure 2.12).

Direction

It is important to be able to show and interpret direction on maps at all scales including atlas maps.

Direction can be expressed in two ways:

- By compass points, for example north or west.

- By compass bearings or angular directions, for example 45°.

Although there are 32 points on a mariner's compass, only 16 are used and shown on maps (Figure 3.2). A **compass bearing** is used to represent the direction of one point relative to another point. Compass bearings are more precise than compass directions because they give exact readings of direction. A bearing is measured in degrees in a clockwise direction from North which is 0°. The bearing of Northeast is 45° while East is 90°. The latter is because east forms a perfect right angle with north. It is best to use a 360° protractor to measure bearings. This enables you to measure every possible bearing without having to move the protractor as you would need to with a 180° protractor.

Likewise, Southeast is 135° and South is 180°. But the real usefulness of bearings is for places which are between these major direction markers. For example, places with bearings of 43°, 49° and 81°. This allows places to be pinpointed with much greater accuracy than compass directions. Look at Figure 3.3 which shows the bearings of the eight major points of the compass. Compass readings can be affected by the presence of iron and steel objects such as pocket knives, belt buckles and railway tracks. Be aware of this when you are taking readings yourself.

The trend of a linear feature, for example a road, or the direction of flow of a river is best expressed by stating opposite compass points. Thus, a road may run from north to south while a river might be flowing from southeast to northwest.

> **Direction:** a line leading to a place or point. Direction is stated by compass points and angular bearings.
>
> **Compass bearing:** direction relative to North as indicated by a compass.

Figure 3.2: 16 points of the compass

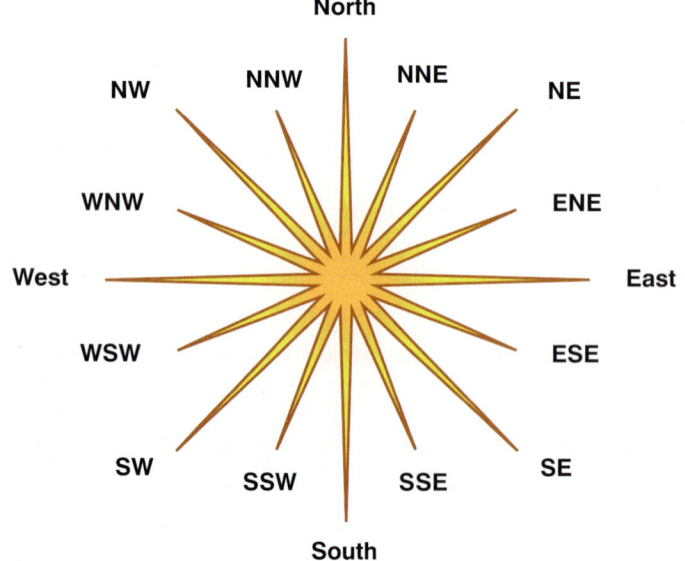

Figure 3.3: Compass bearings

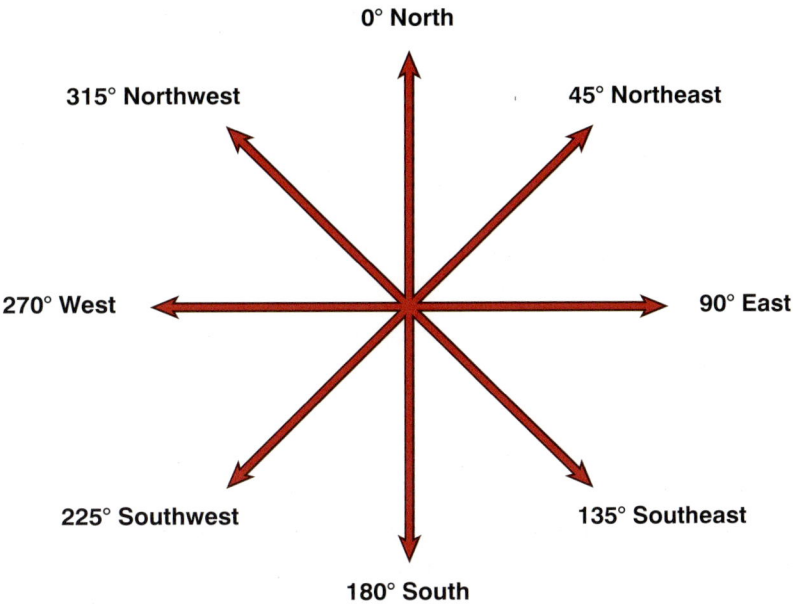

Activities 3.1

1. Give the opposite directions to the following:

   (a) northeast; (b) north-northwest; (c) west-southwest; (d) southeast; (e) northeast.

2. What do the following direction abbreviations mean: (a) NNE; (b) ESE; (c) NE; (d) SSW?

3. (a) What is a compass bearing?

   (b) How is a compass bearing measured?

4. Use Figure 3.3 to help you calculate the bearings for the eight subsidiary points of the compass.

The global geographic grid system

> **Latitude:** an imaginary line (a circle) around the earth running parallel to the Equator. It is the angular distance north or south from the Equator.
>
> **Longitude:** imaginary lines drawn through the North and South Poles, used to measure distance east and west. Greenwich, England, is designated as 0°, with other distances being measured east and west of Greenwich.

Any place on the earth's surface can be located exactly by its **latitude** and **longitude** (Figure 3.4). The **Equator** divides the world into the northern hemisphere and the southern hemisphere. Every point on the Equator is exactly half-way between the North Pole and the South Pole. Lines of latitude are parallel to the Equator. This is why lines of latitude are sometimes called 'parallels'! On a world map they run from west to east. They decrease in diameter from the Equator to the poles.

There are five major circles of latitude. These are the Equator, the tropics of Cancer and Capricorn, and the Arctic and Antarctic circles. The **Tropic of Cancer** (23½°N) is the most northerly position where the sun shines directly down onto the earth's surface at an angle of 90°. This occurs at the summer solstice in the Northern Hemisphere on 21st June. The **Tropic of Capricorn** (23½°S) is the most southerly position where the sun shines directly down on the earth's surface at an angle of 90°. This occurs on the 21st December, the date of the winter solstice in the Northern Hemisphere, but the summer solstice in the Southern Hemisphere.

During summer in the Northern Hemisphere the duration of daylight hours increases towards the North Pole. It reaches daylight for a whole 24 hour period on 21st June at 66½°N. This is the significance of the **Arctic Circle**. In the southern hemisphere, the **Antarctic Circle** plays the same role. The number of whole days with continuous daylight steadily increases in summer from the Arctic Circle to the North Pole. While this is happening in the northern hemisphere the reverse occurs between the Antarctic Circle and the South Pole.

Because the earth is a sphere, its circumference decreases from the Equator to the poles. At the Equator the circumference is 40,075 km. At the Arctic Circle it has been reduced to 17,602 km, about 44% of the circumference at the Equator.

Latitude, like longitude, is measured in degrees, minutes and seconds. The Equator is at 0°. The North Pole is 90° north. This is because lines from the North Pole and the Equator meeting at the centre of the earth form at an angle of 90°. The South Pole is 90° south for the same reason. If a place is 45° north it is because lines from that place and from the Equator meeting at the centre of the earth form an angle of 45°.

One degree of latitude covers a distance of 111 km. Because this is quite a long distance, a degree of latitude is divided into sections known as minutes. There are 60 minutes in a degree. Thus the latitude of Kingston, Jamaica is 18° 0 minutes North while London, UK is 51° 30 minutes North. A minute measures 1.85 km. For an absolutely precise location seconds are also used. A minute is divided into 60 seconds. A second measures 31 metres.

Figure 3.4: Lines of latitude and longitude

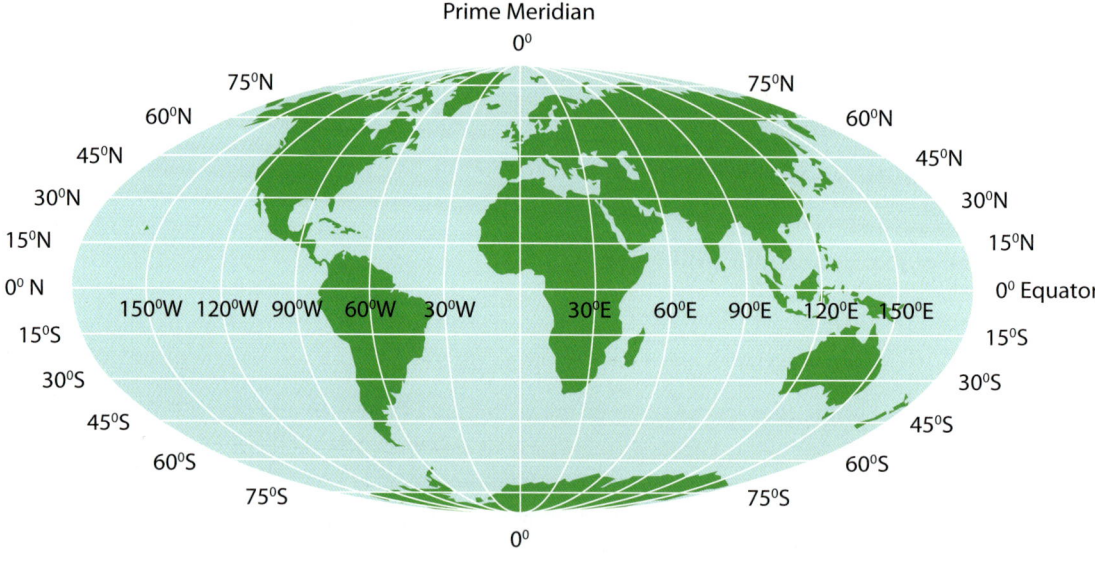

Lines of longitude (or meridians) link the north and south poles. They are at right angles to the Equator. As the Equator is the main point of reference for latitude, Greenwich, UK provides a similar function for longitude. The line of longitude which passes through the old Royal Observatory in Greenwich is known as the **Prime Meridian** (0° longitude). The longitude of any other place is referred to as being east or west of Greenwich. It is measured by an angle at the centre of the earth from the Prime Meridian. Because longitude circles the whole of the globe, the maximum longitude is 180°. This will be on the opposite side of the world to Greenwich.

When the position of a place is given, latitude is always stated first, followed by longitude. Thus, the location of Addis Ababa, the capital city of Ethiopia, is 9° 45 minutes North and 40° 30 minutes East.

Activities 3.2

1. Give the latitudes of (a) the Equator; (b) the Tropic of Cancer; (c) the Tropic of Capricorn; (d) the Arctic Circle; (e) the Antarctic Circle.

2. Briefly state the significance of each of these five points.

3. Give the global positions of (a) Tokyo; (b) New York; (c) Moscow; (d) Beijing.

Longitude and time zones

Photo 3.2

Daylight occurs when a place on the earth's surface is facing the sun. When a place is facing away from the sun it is night. The earth rotates on its axis (makes a full turn) once every 24 hours. One rotation makes a circle of 360°. This means that it moves 15° every hour (24 x 15 = 360).

Thus, the world is divided into 24 standard **time zones** (Figure 3.5). Each is centred on lines of longitude at 15° intervals. The Greenwich Meridian is at the centre of the first zone. All places to the west of Greenwich are one hour behind for every 15° of longitude. Places to the east are ahead by one hour for every 15°.

For the population of the earth the sun rises in the morning in the east. Its angle is very low at first but gradually it becomes higher in the sky. When the sun reaches its highest position in the sky over a place it is said to be 12.00 **Local Time** along this line of longitude. When the sun is highest in the sky at Greenwich it is 12.00 noon **Greenwich Mean Time** or G.M.T. After noon the angle of the sun declines until sunset. The sun sets in the west.

Most countries have just one time zone. This means it is the same time everywhere in the country. However some countries are so wide, covering many degrees of longitude, that they need more than one time zone. Russia has eleven and Canada has six.

Figure 3.5: Longitude and time zones

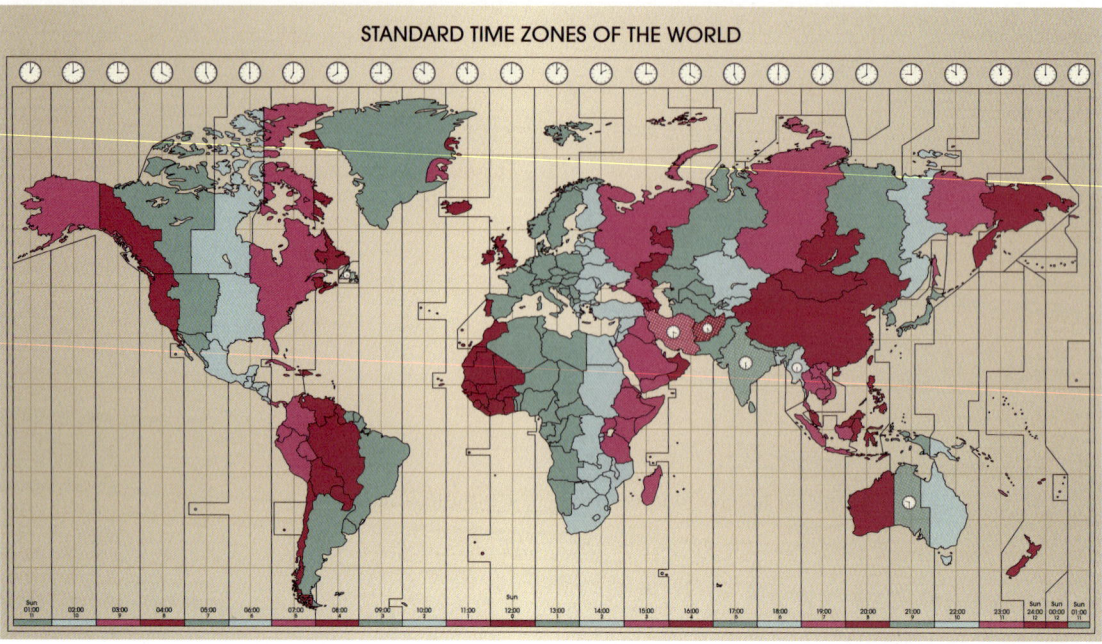

National grid systems

All countries use a **national grid system** for their own maps. This means that every individual place in the country will have its own particular grid reference. One of the most famous mapping agencies in the world is the Ordnance Survey of Great Britain which has produced the British national grid reference system. National grid reference systems are different from using latitude and longitude. The Ordnance Survey's system is widely used in their survey data and in their published maps. Grid references are also commonly quoted in other publications and data sources such as government planning documents and guide books.

Figure 3.6: National grid reference system for Great Britain

				HP		
			HT	HU		
	HW	HX	HY	HZ		
NA	NB	NC	ND			
NF	NG	NH	NJ	NK		
NL	NM	NN	NO			
	NR	NS	NT	NU		
	NW	NX	NY	NZ	OV	
		SC	SD	SE	TA	
		SH	SJ	SK	TF	TG
	SM	SN	SO	SP	TL	TM
	SR	SS	ST	SU	TQ	TR
SV	SW	SX	SY	SZ	TV	

Source: Wiki Commons, National Grid for Great Britain

Figure 3.6 shows the national grid reference system for Great Britain. The **national grid origin** (or starting point for the grid) is in the south-western most corner of the country. Most countries follow this system. For the first letter of each square the grid is divided into squares of size 500 km by 500 km. There are four of these which contain significant land area within Great Britain: S, T, N and H. Notice that the southwest of the country begins with 'S'; the Southeast with 'T'; the Northeast with 'N'; and the northwest with 'N' or 'H'.

For the second letter, each large square is subdivided into 25 squares of size 100 km by 100 km, each with a letter code from A to Z (omitting I), starting with A in the north-west corner to Z in the south-east corner. Figure 3.6 shows the resultant grid, with the squares containing land lettered, and the central meridian marked in red.

Activities 3.3

1. Give the global position of the ferry port of Holyhead on Holy Island.

2. Approximately how far is Cardiff from Anglesey?

3. Describe the altitude of the Cambrian Mountains.

Weather maps, including synoptic charts

> **Synoptic scale:** In meteorology the synoptic scale (also known as large scale or cyclonic scale) is a distance of 1000 km or more. This corresponds to the scale typical of depressions and anticyclones in mid-latitudes.

A competent student of geography should have a reasonable degree of confidence in interpreting weather maps. Weather maps come in a variety of shapes and sizes. You only have to look at the weather forecasts in a range of newspapers to see that some weather maps are very simplistic while others show a much greater degree of detail.

The Meteorological (Met) Office is the primary source of weather forecasts in the UK. The most comprehensive weather maps are known as synoptic charts which show the atmospheric conditions of an area at a particular time. The Met Office produces charts each day for the main synoptic hours – midnight, 6.00am, midday, and 6.00pm. Figure 3.7 shows the official weather symbols used on synoptic charts. Data is gathered from a large network of both manned and automatic weather stations to provide detailed forecasts.

Figure 3.7: Weather symbols

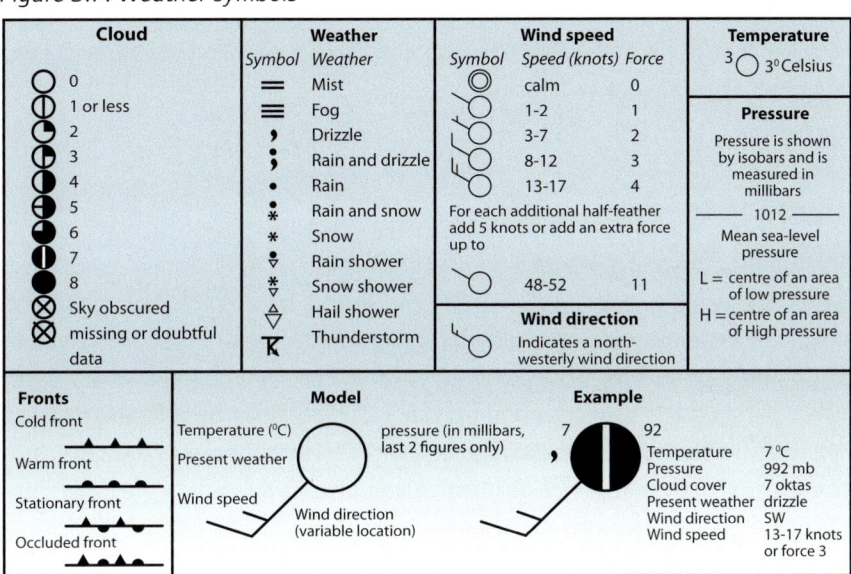

Figure 3.8: Synoptic chart showing an anticyclone over the UK and Ireland

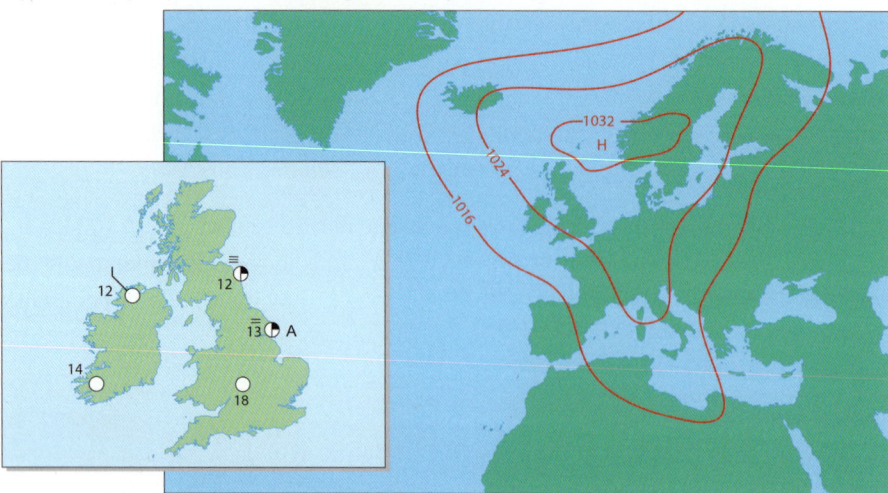

Source: Geographical Enquiries, Nelson Thornes

Isobars are the main feature on a synoptic chart. Figure 3.8 shows an anticyclone or large high pressure system over the UK and Republic of Ireland. Isobars are isolines joining places of equal pressure as discussed earlier in this section of the book. The average sea level pressure over the UK is 1013 mb (millibars), so the isobars on Figure 3.8 are well over this level. The large letter 'H' reinforces the fact that this is a substantial area of high pressure. In addition to the isobars, information is also plotted for a selected number of weather stations. Each weather station is indicated by a circle. By consulting Figure 3.7, the table of weather symbols, you can see that for weather station A:

- The temperature is 13°C;
- The cloud cover is 3/8 (three oktas);
- The precipitation situation is misty;
- The pressure is between 1024 and 1032 mb;
- There is no recorded wind speed or direction.

Anticyclones generally bring calm weather which in summer can be hot and sunny, but in winter cold, frosty and foggy. In an anticyclone air is subsiding in the atmosphere. When it reaches the surface it blows outwards from the centre of the anticyclone in a clockwise direction. Sometimes large high pressure systems can remain in the same general location for many days or even weeks. When this occurs they are referred to as blocking anticyclones because they block the normal path of depressions coming in from the Atlantic Ocean.

Figure 3.9 shows a very different weather situation. Now a large depression, which is in the process of occlusion, is over the UK and Ireland. You should be able to recognise three types of front which are boundaries between different air masses. These are:

- The warm front.
- The cold front.
- The occluded front.

The warm front is the leading part of a depression as these weather systems cross the Atlantic Ocean from west to east. The area between the warm front and the cold front at the back of the system is known as the warm sector. Temperatures are higher in the warm sector than in the air ahead of the warm front and behind the cold front. Notice how the occluded front typically curls around the centre of low pressure. Occlusion occurs when a depression is beginning to fizzle out. The occluded front is where the cold and warm fronts have merged as the faster moving cold front has caught up with the slower moving warm front and the warm air in that part of the warm sector has been lifted off the ground. It then continues to rise up in the atmosphere gradually mixing with the air around it until eventually there is no difference and therefore no front. This process 'travels down' the warm sector until the whole depression eventually dissipates.

Figure 3.9: Synoptic chart showing a depression (low pressure system) over the UK and Ireland

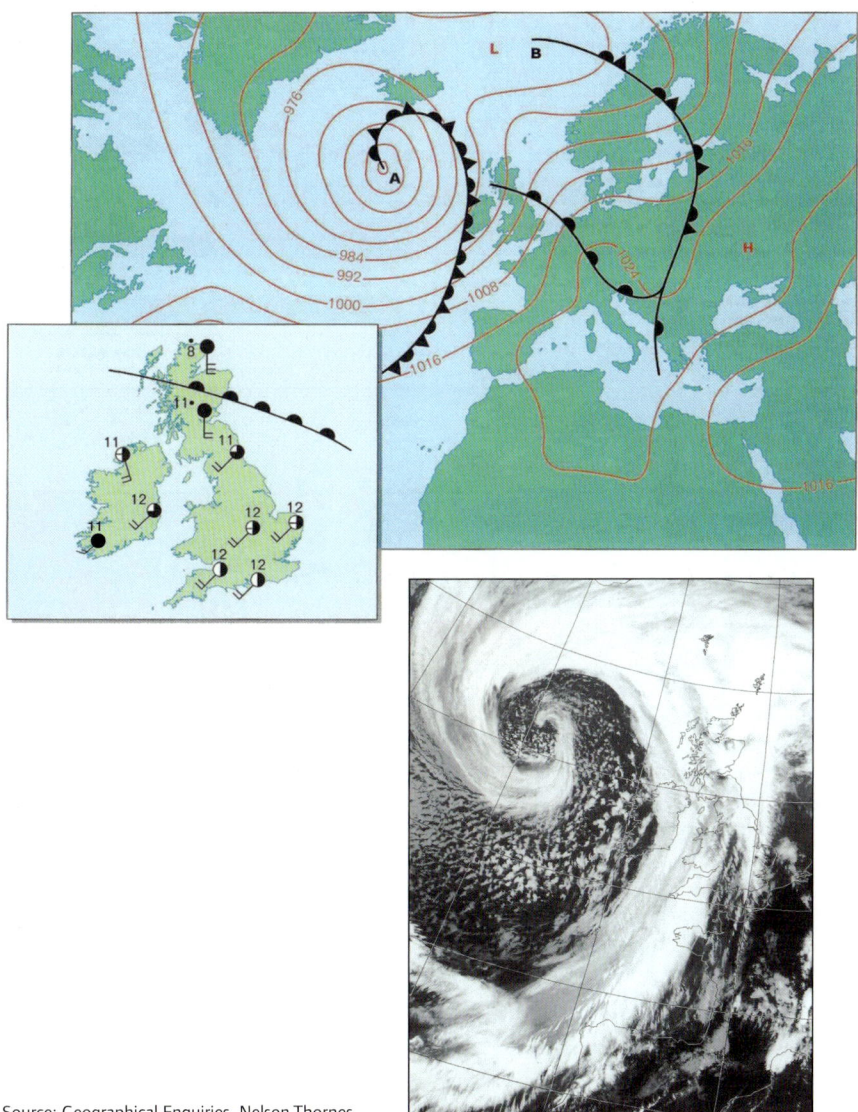

Source: Geographical Enquiries, Nelson Thornes

You can see that the lowest pressure of 984 mb is well below the average for the UK, so this is a significant depression. The occurrence of the letter 'L' (for 'Low') reinforces that this is the centre of the weather system. Notice that the pressure rises as you move away from the centre of a depression. This is the opposite situation to an anticyclone. Also the isobars are much closer together in a depression indicating a higher pressure gradient resulting in higher wind speeds. Air is drawn into a depression in an anticlockwise direction with air rising along the fronts to create cloud and precipitation. Because the angle of the warm front in the atmosphere is lower than that of the cold front the former brings a longer period of rain, but it is generally not so blustery as that along the cold front. The steeper cold front brings more intense rainfall. Occluded fronts usually bring a long period of rain which is slow to clear.

Again, information for a selected number of weather stations is included on the synoptic chart of a depression. Compared to an anticyclone notice:

● The much greater levels of cloud cover.

● The high incidence of precipitation.

● The stronger winds.

● The difference in wind direction.

● The difference in pressure and the steeper pressure gradient.

By studying synoptic charts we can see how different weather conditions affect daily weather events. The more you look at synoptic charts, particularly if you follow the tracks of depressions and anticyclones across the Atlantic Ocean the more you will be able to recognise and understand basic weather systems and the sequence of weather they bring.

Figure 3.10 is a cross-section diagram of a typical depression which should be viewed in conjunction with the depression shown on the synoptic chart. Looking at both illustrations together helps to clarify what is actually happening in the atmosphere.

Figure 3.10: A cross-section of a typical depression

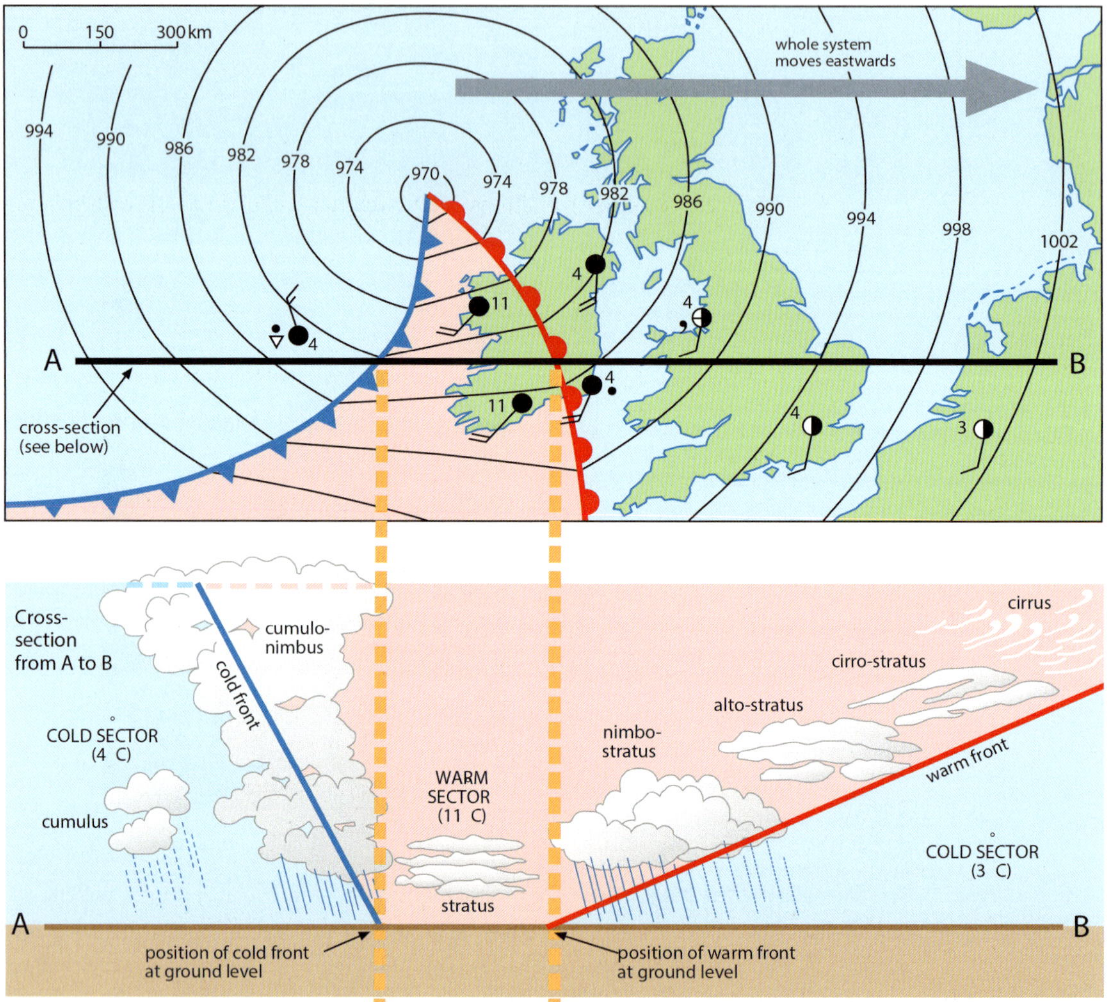

	after cold front	as cold front passes	warm sector	as warm front passes over	as warm front approaches	well before warm front
cloud type	fair weather cumulus	towering cumulo-nimbus	dull, low, flat stratus	dense nimbo-stratus	lower, thicker alto-stratus	high altitude cirrus and cirro-stratus
rainfall	isolated scattered showers	heavy showers	mainly dry	moderate rain	drizzle	no rain
temp.(°C)	4°C	4°C	11°C	4°C	4°C	3°C
wind	north-west, getting weaker	north-west, strong, gusty	south-west, steady, strong	southerly, strong	southerly, light, getting stronger	southerly, light
air pressure	rising	rising	steady	falling	1002 – 998 falling	high (1002),falling

Activities 3.4

1. What is meant by synoptic scale?

2. When are the main synoptic hours?

3. Look at Figure 3.8:

   (a) Describe the location of the centre of the anticyclone.

   (b) How far south does the 1016 mb isobar stretch?

   (c) Describe the weather at the weather station located in northeast England.

4. Look at Figure 3.9:

   (a) Where is the centre of the depression located?

   (b) In which direction is the depression moving?

   (c) What is the overall pattern of wind direction?

   (d) Describe the weather conditions at the weather station in southwest Ireland.

Maps with located proportional symbols

> **Proportional symbol maps:** A cartographic tool to assist in the visualisation and analysis of quantitative data associated with specific locations. The area of each symbol is proportional to the value represented.

In this cartographic technique the symbols drawn are proportional in size to the size of the factor being represented. For example, the symbol representing a settlement of 10,000 people should be ten times larger than the symbol for a settlement of 1,000 people. A wide variety of different symbols could be used, for example the symbol of a person could be used to indicate the size of a population. However, the specification itemises only the most widely used types of symbol – circles, semi-circles, squares and bars.

Proportional circles and semi-circles

Figure 3.11: An example of a choropleth with proportional circles

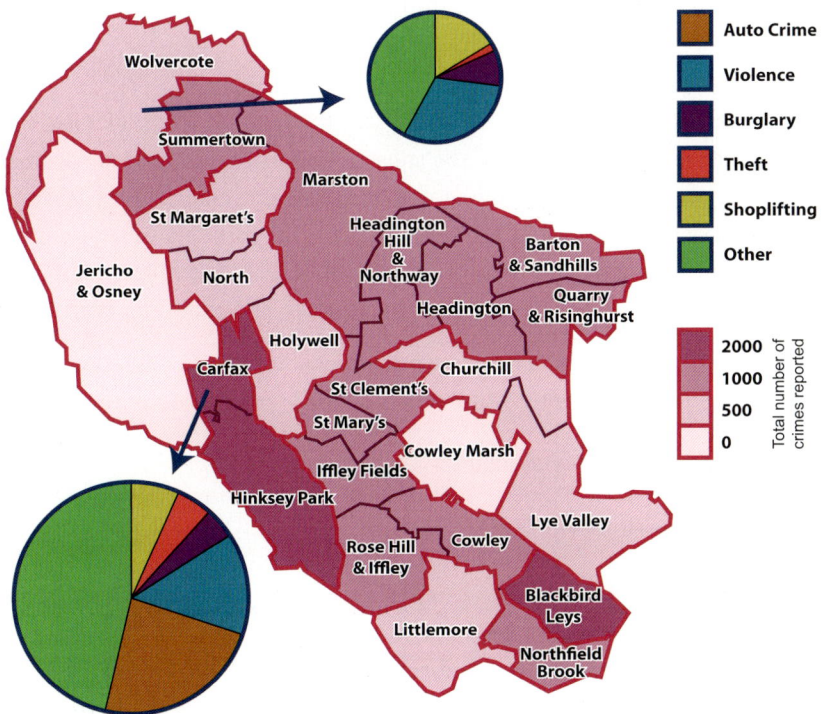

Proportional circles are the next step up from pie charts. While pie charts are viewed as a basic graphical technique, proportional circles are a higher level technique. Proportional circles are useful when illustrating the differences between two or more amounts. They are particularly effective when placed on location maps. In Figure 3.11 the two circles shown are proportional in area to the total number of offences recorded in the two urban areas. It is most desirable to place the symbols inside the boundaries of the regions the values refer to. However, if some symbols cannot fit comfortably within their regions place them in the nearest comfortable space and use 'leader lines' to connect them with their regions. The method used to decide the radius of each circle is as follows:

- Write out each of the total figures for which circles are to be drawn in the first column.

- Find the square root for each figure and write it down in the second column

- Use the square root for the radius of each circle. By doing this the area of each of the circles will be mathematically proportional to the figures they are representing. For the radii you can use any units you want providing they are the same for each of the circles.

Figure 3.12 shows a very simple example of how to calculate the relative sizes of three proportional circles.

Figure 3.12: Calculating the size of proportional circles

Totals	Square root	Radius of circle
4	2	2 cm
9	3	3 cm
16	4	4 cm

Circles can be divided into sectors to provide more detailed information. For example, in Figure 3.11 the two proportional circles are sub-divided into the six different types of crime. In this way the technique is able to convey a significant amount of information in a visually impressive form.

Proportional semi-circles can be used to show two sets of data. When carefully constructed with contrasting colouring/shading and a clear key, this can be a good technique to use, particularly when there is a lot of data to illustrate.

Create a number of symbols for round numbers near the bottom, middle and top of your range of values for a key. Remember to use the square roots to calculate symbol sizes, but label them with the original values.

Proportional squares and bars

Proportional squares are constructed in a similar way to proportional circles. Here the square root value is used to decide the length of the side of the square. Proportional squares are positioned in as central a position as possible over the area they represent. If two squares overlap it is possible to lighten the shading of one square for the purposes of clarity. As with circles, proportional squares can also be sub-divided (Figure 3.13). In this example, the proportional squares show the relative population sizes of three countries with the proportion of the population that is urban also shown for each country.

With **proportional bars** the length of a bar is proportional to the value it represents. Again, bars can be divided to illustrate a number of different categories.

Figure 3.13: Sub-divided proportional squares

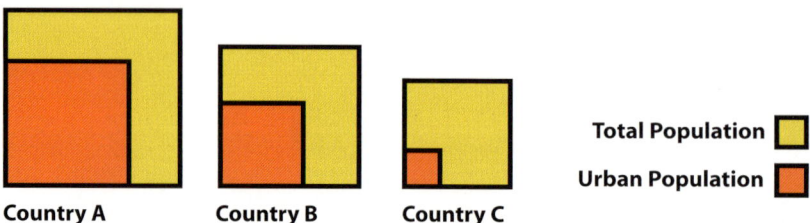

Country A   Country B   Country C

Total Population
Urban Population

Maps showing movement

Flow maps are used to show the movement of goods, traffic, people and information between places. Flow lines, desire lines and trip lines are all used to illustrate the volume and direction of movement from place to place. The most basic of these techniques is the use of trip lines which uses uniformly thin and straight lines to link points of origin and destination. For example, trip lines might be drawn to show where shoppers in a market town live. Such a trip line map might link 20 villages in the surrounding area to the market town, each link being shown by a thin straight line. Invariably some lines will be short and others much longer in length.

Figure 3.14: Flow line diagram

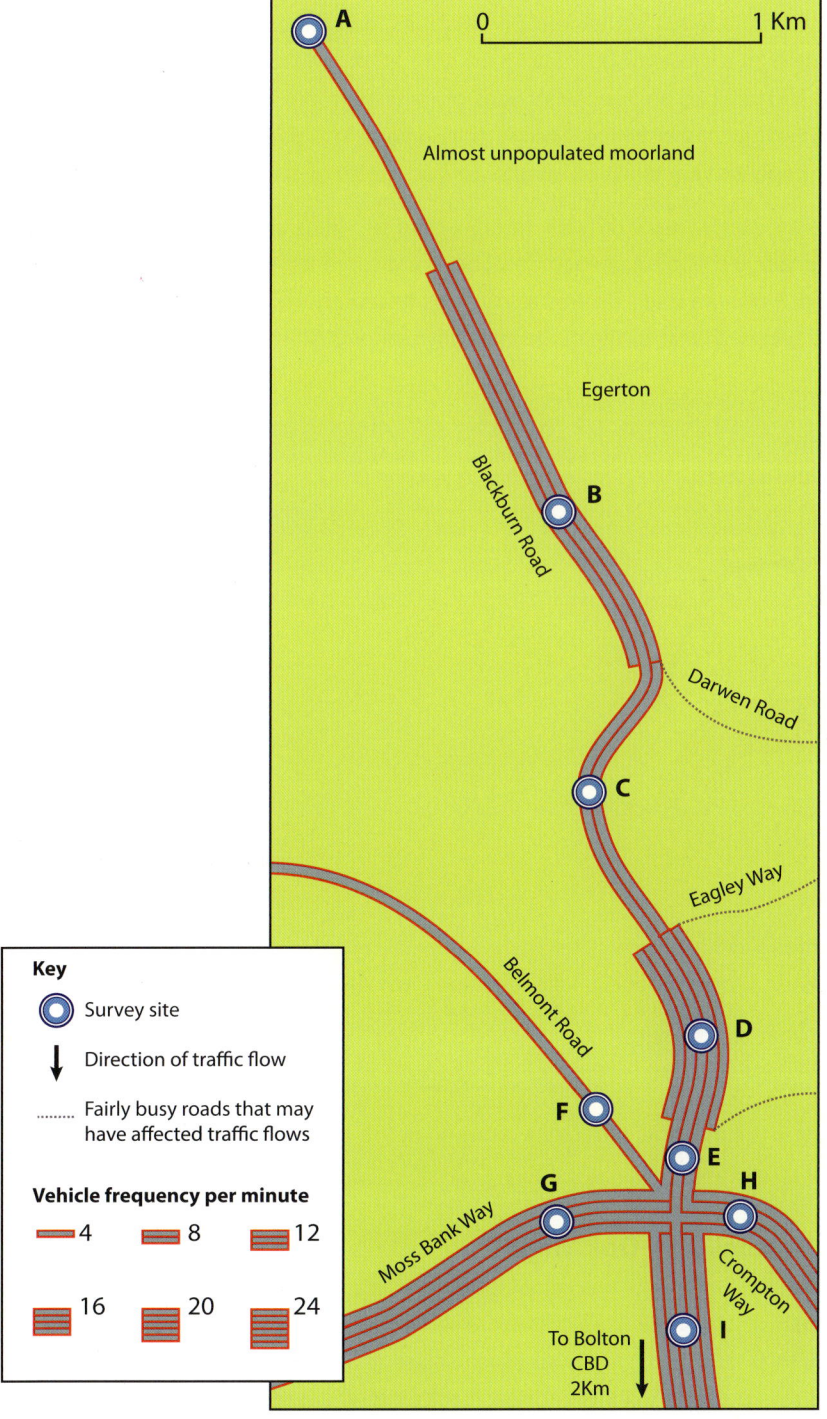

Source: Adapted from Geographical Enquiries, Nelson Thornes

In contrast to trip lines, flow line and desire line diagrams use lines which are proportional to the volume of movement. The difference between the latter two is that flow lines follow actual routes while desire lines are drawn directly from the point of origin to the point of destination. Desire lines are particularly effective in showing direction of movement and can be impressive when superimposed on a base map. Desire lines are often used to show:

● migrations of populations both within and between countries.

● trade between countries.

● tourism.

● water flow.

Flow lines (Figure 3.14) might be used to show the different volumes of traffic from different smaller settlements into a larger settlement or variations in volume of traffic within an urban area. Thus, a line 10mm wide may represent 500 vehicles an hour along a road. On the same scale a line 2mm wide would represent 100 vehicles an hour. Directions of movement are indicated by arrows. Flow lines could also be used to show the number of buses coming into a town for a particular day. The success of using proportional flow lines depends very much on an appropriate choice of scale.

Flow lines are clearly more difficult to draw than trip lines and desire lines. The best method is to use a 'guide line' along the route of each flow line as indicated in Figure 3.15. For any one line insert bars of the correct width using a ruler. Do this as often as necessary, moving along the guide line and rotating your bars to be perpendicular to the guide line. Now connect all the outer ends of the bars.

Figure 3.15: Constructing a flow line

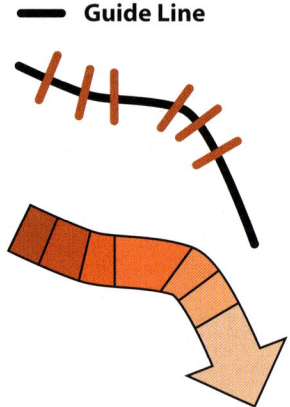

— **Bars**
— **Guide Line**

Activities 3.5

1. Construct three proportional circles using the data in Figure 3.12.

2. (a) What are trip lines?

   (b) Give an example of how a trip line diagram might be used.

3. What is the essential difference between desire lines and flow lines?

Choropleth, Isolines and Dot Maps

Choropleth maps

A choropleth (Figure 3.16) is a map which shows relative density per area. Areas are coloured or shaded according to a prearranged key with each colour or shading representing a range of values. Choropleth maps can use variations in colour or different densities of black and white shading. This technique is good for showing comparisons between places. The base maps for choropleth maps show regions or areas such as the boroughs in London or the counties in England. The following steps should be followed in the construction of a choropleth map:

● Find a good, clear base map.

● Look at the range of data and divide it into classes. There should be no less than four classes and no more than eight. In the former case, there would not be enough variation on the map and in the latter situation the map would contain so much information that it could be confusing to many people.

● Ensure that the class or category values do not overlap, i.e. 0-19.9, 20-39.9., 40-59.9.

● Allocate a colour or density shading to each class. The convention is that shading gets darker as values increase.

● Now apply each colour to the applicable areas of the map.

● Provide a key, scale and north point.

Examples of the use of choropleth maps include:

● The number of crimes recorded for local authority areas in a town or city.

● The unemployment rate by region in a country.

● Population density by country on a map of Europe.

● Variations in land use such as the amount of recreational land or the type of forest cover.

Figure 3.16: A choropleth map showing fertility rates in Europe

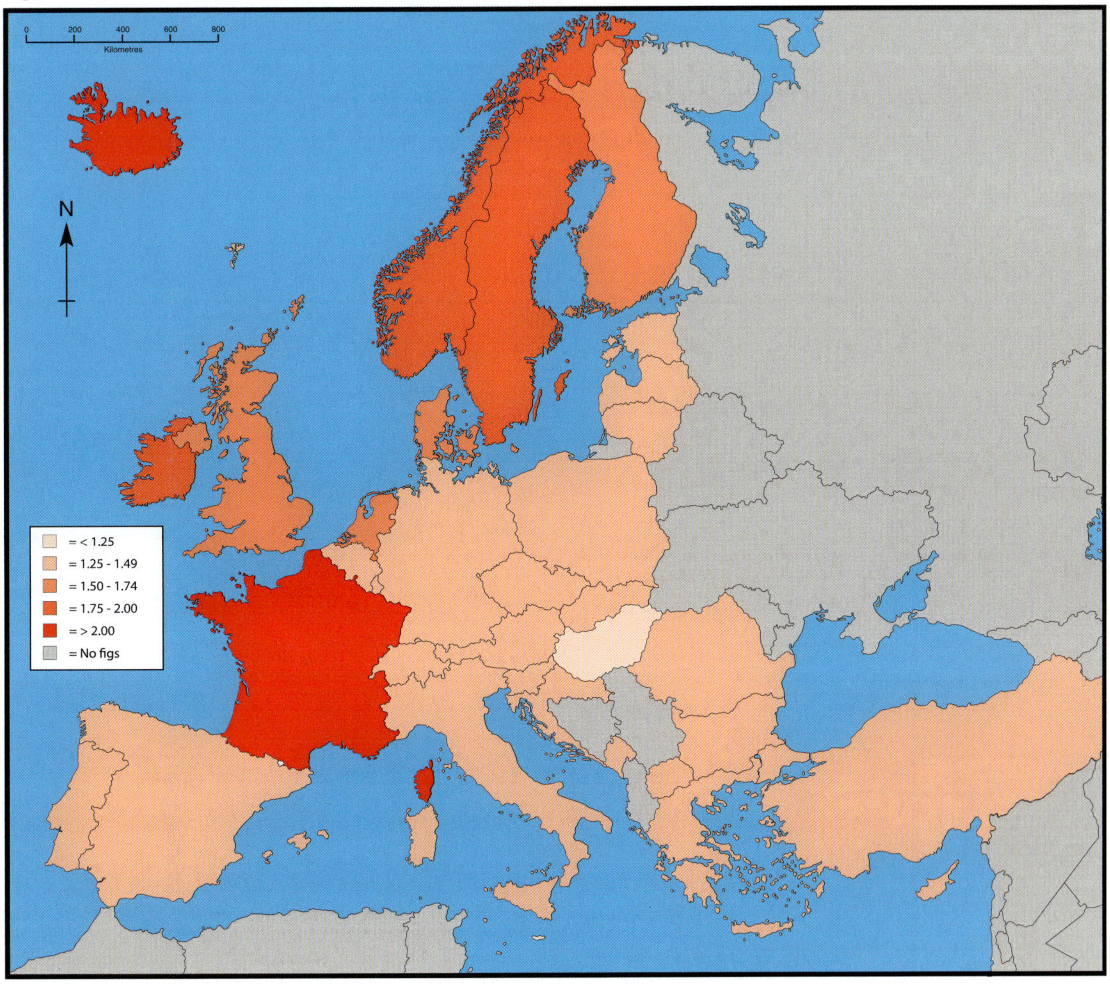

Source: Based on 2011 figures from Eurostat

The choropleth is a popular technique, frequently used in atlases, textbooks and many other types of publication. It can convey a considerable amount of information in a straightforward and visually appealing way. The main disadvantage of the choropleth is that it can show abrupt changes at boundary lines when in reality change is much more gradual. It also gives the impression of uniformity within individual areas on the map when in reality a reasonable degree of variation may be present. Careful selection of class sizes can reduce this problem.

Isoline diagrams

Isolines join points of equal value on a map. They are similar to contours on an Ordnance Survey map which join points of equal height. Isolines can only be drawn when the values under consideration change in a fairly gradual way over the area of the map. Data for quite a large number of locations is required in order to draw a good isoline map. If the data available is patchy or the spatial distribution is complex and disjointed, this technique is difficult to apply as too much guesswork is involved.

Usually a fixed interval is selected, such as the contour interval on an Ordnance Survey map, so that the reader can sense how quickly a phenomenon changes even without looking closely at the figures. An isoline passes between values that are higher and lower so that all values on one side of the line will be higher, and all those to the other side will be lower. The space between different value isolines can be coloured or shaded as in the way that relief is illustrated in atlas maps. If colouring or shading is used then a key should be included.

Isolines are a good technique for showing gradual change over an area. They avoid the abrupt effect which boundary lines produce on a choropleth map. Drawing isolines allows the data to be used to describe the whole area under consideration rather than just reflecting on a series of points because they allow a pattern to be seen in a distribution.

Figure 3.17 is an isoline map showing daily average sulphur dioxide concentrations ($\mu g/m^3$) in Northern Bohemia, Czech Republic during a winter smog event. You can see that visual estimation is an important part of constructing a good isoline map. Isolines can be particularly effective when superimposed on a base map.

Figure 3.17: An isoline map

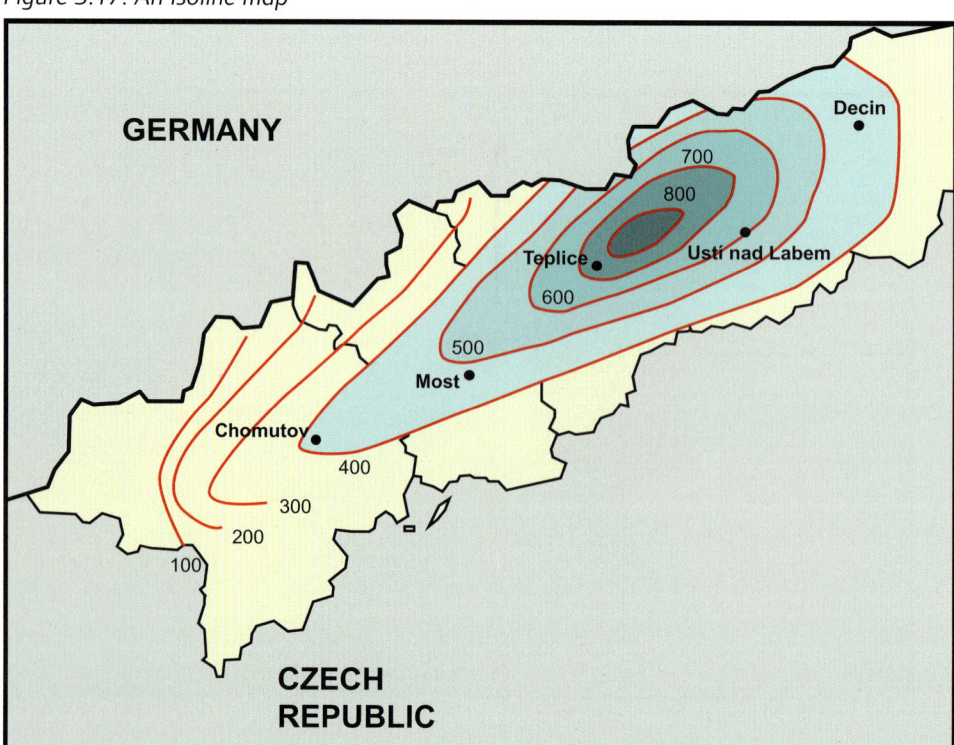

Isolines are also typically used to represent:

- Air pressure in the form of isobars.
- Temperature in the form of isotherms.
- Rainfall in the form of isohyets.
- Lines of equal travel time in the form of isochrones.
- Noise contours around an airport.
- Pedestrian densities in a CBD.
- Variations in house prices in urban areas.

Dot maps

Dot maps (Figure 3.18) are used to illustrate the distribution of phenomena such as population, houses or plants by creating a visual impression of density. The pattern of dots can also be analysed statistically, for example by nearest neighbour analysis.

Two parameters must be initially considered; the graphical size of each dot and the value associated with each dot. The dot value should be carefully chosen so that it is high enough to avoid excessive overcrowding of dots in areas with a high concentration of the variable, but low enough to prevent areas with low concentrations having no dots at all which could give a false impression of emptiness. Ideally, dots should not merge. Dots are positioned on the map to show as closely as possible the distribution of the variable being mapped. Figure 3.18 is a dot map showing the population distribution of the United States in 2010 with each dot representing 7,500 people. The map shows clearly the locations of densely and sparsely populated areas.

Different coloured dots can be used when the subject under consideration has sub-divisions, for example different ethnic groups in a population or different types of trees in a region.

Figure 3.18: A dot map showing the distribution of population in the United States in 2010

One dot = 7500 people

Source: United States Census Bureau

The main advantage of choosing to use a dot map is that it can be very effective in providing a good visual impression of variations in spatial distributions providing the dots are carefully positioned. To do this you need detailed information before you start to construct a map of this kind. However, large numbers of dots are difficult to count and thus it can be difficult to try to estimate actual figures in terms of say the population of a densely populated area.

Activities 3.6

1. (a) Briefly describe the variations in total fertility rates shown by Figure 3.16, a choropleth map.

   (b) What is the main disadvantage of choropleth maps?

2. Briefly describe the pattern of concentration of sulphur dioxide in Figure 3.17, an isoline map.

Chapter 4

Graphical skills

Line and bar graphs

Line graphs

Line graphs are relatively simple graphs which show, for example, change over time. Line graphs use continuous data and they show trends. These trends can be absolute or they can be relative. Line graphs can be simple – showing one feature – or they can be multiple – showing many features.

In all line graphs there is an independent and dependent variable. In the climate graph of Kingston, Jamaica (Figure 4.1), the months of the year are the independent variable whereas the temperature and rainfall are the dependent variables. They depend on the season. Note that the rainfall is shown as a set of bars – one for each month's rainfall whereas the temperature is shown as a line graph.

Figure 4.1: Climate graph for Kingston, Jamaica

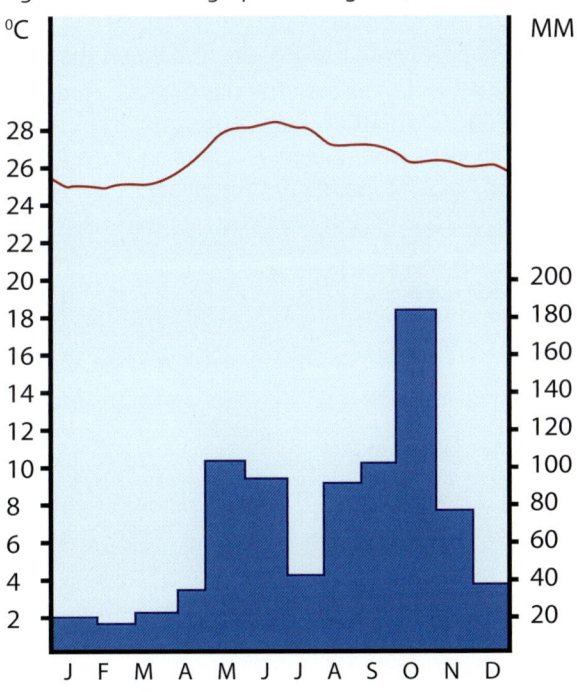

Source: Earth Trends

Figure 4.2: Divergent line graph showing energy consumption in Zimbabwe

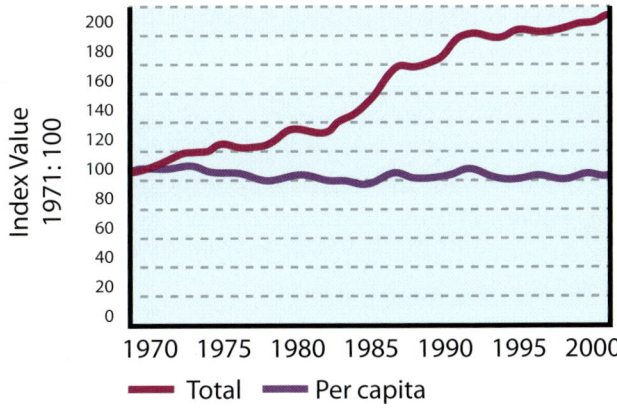

Source: Earth Trends

Figure 4.2 shows energy consumption in Zimbabwe, 1971-99. This is a divergent line graph, which shows changes in two aspects compared with 1971 levels. In contrast, Figure 4.3 is a compound line graph which shows energy consumption by source in Zimbabwe for 1971-99. This type of graph often confuses students as the values for all features apart from the bottom one (i.e. Other renewables (fuelwood) and Hydroelectric) begin at points above 0. In Figure 4.3, the values for 'Hydroelectric are shown above fossil fuels and 'Other renewables' are shown above Hydroelectric'.

Figure 4.3: Compound line graph showing energy consumption by source in Zimbabwe

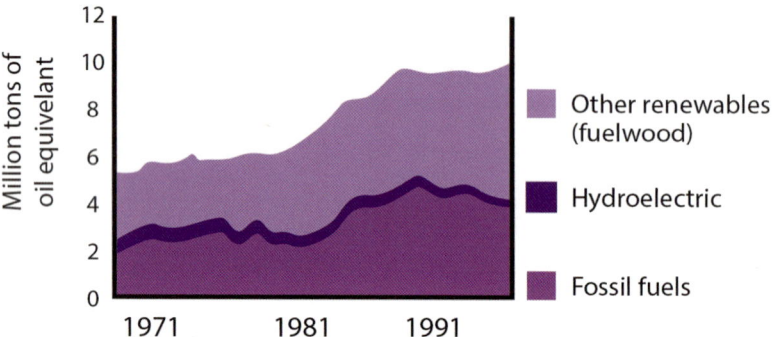

A **comparative line graph** is used to compare two or more sets of data on the same axis, as shown in Figure 4.4. The graph was produced in 2015 and so values after this date are predictions.

Figure 4.4: A comparative line graph to show trends in Global FDI (foreign direct investment) by groups of economies, 2005-2015, and projections to 2018 (values in US$ billions)

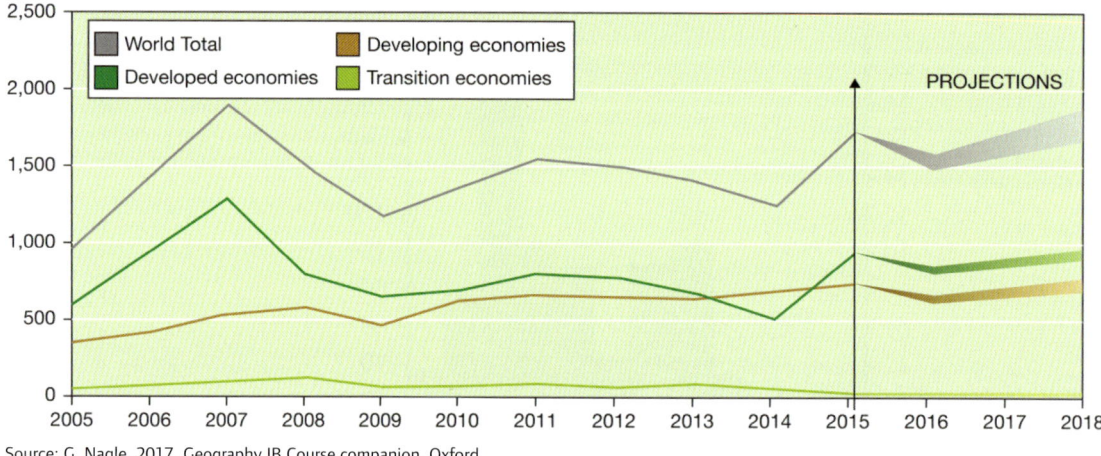

Source: G. Nagle, 2017, Geography IB Course companion, Oxford

Bar charts

Bar charts are one of the simplest ways of presenting data. In bar charts the length of each bar represents the quantity of each component, e.g. places or time intervals. The vertical axis has a scale which measures the total of each of these components. There are four main types of bar chart, as follows.

- **Simple bar chart** – each bar indicates a single factor. If the difference in the length of the bars is not great, then differences can be emphasised by leaving a space between them or by 'breaking' the vertical scale. The rainfall for Kingston (Figure 4.1) contains a simple bar chart, as well as a line graph. Figure 4.5 is a bar graph showing the biggest aquaculture producers in 2009. It is convention to have the bars either in descending order, or, as in the case here, ascending order.

- **Comparative (multiple or group) bar chart** – features are grouped together on one graph to help comparison or to show changing frequencies in a variable over time. Figure 4.6 is a comparative bar graph showing the Tata Group's revenue by source and year.

- **Compound or component bar chart** – various elements or factors are grouped together on one bar (the most stable element or factor is placed at the bottom to avoid disturbance). A **percentage compound** or **component bar chart** is a variation on the compound bar chart. It is used to compare features by showing the percentage contribution. These graphs do not give a total in each category, but compare relative changes in percentages.

- **Divergent bar chart** – these show positive and negative changes in a set of data.

Figure 4.5: Bar graph to show biggest aqua-culture producers, 2009

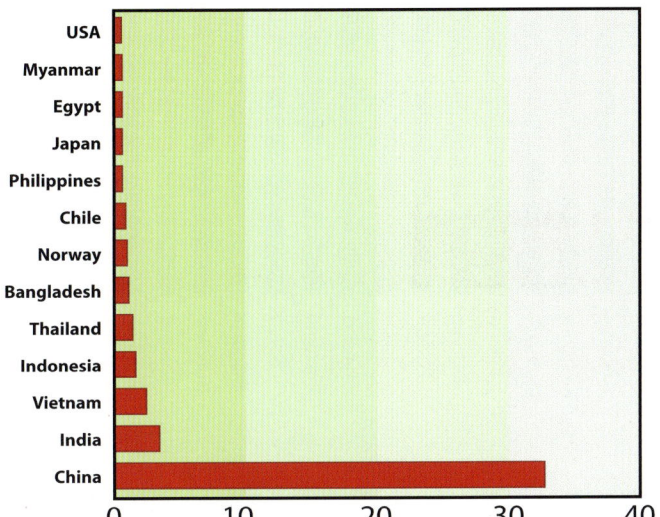

One widely used variant of the multiple bar chart (histogram) is the age-sex pyramid. This is constructed in 1, 5 or 10-year age groups with males on one side and females on the other. This almost always takes the form of a pyramid, with the youngest age group at the base and the oldest at the top. The horizontal bars are drawn proportional in length to either the percentage of the total population or the actual number in each group.

Figure 4.6: The Tata Group's revenue by source and year

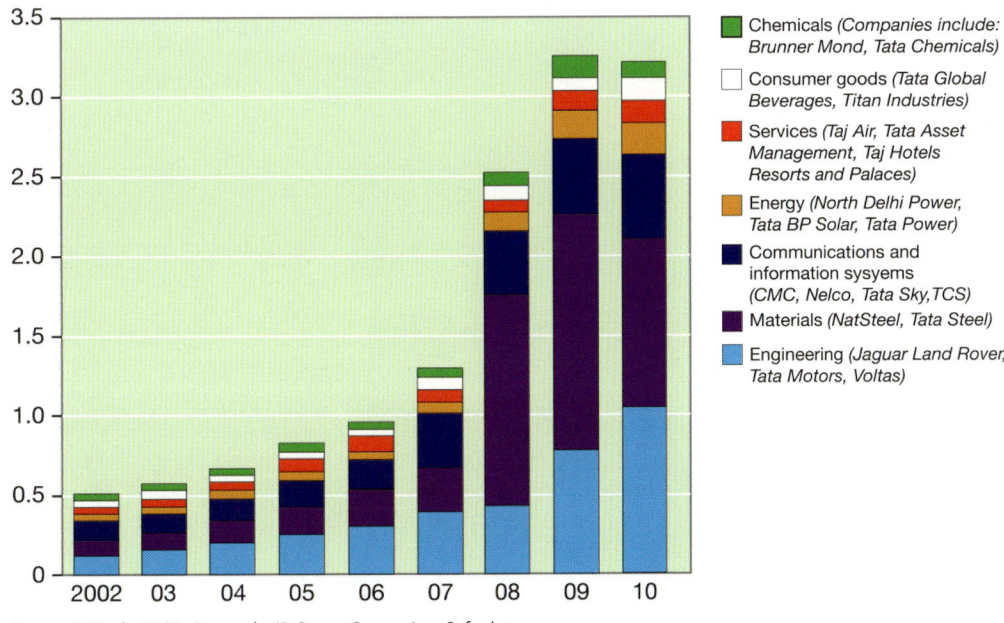

Source: G. Nagle, 2017, Geography IB Course Companion, Oxford

Figure 4.7: A compound bar graph showing waste management in the European Union

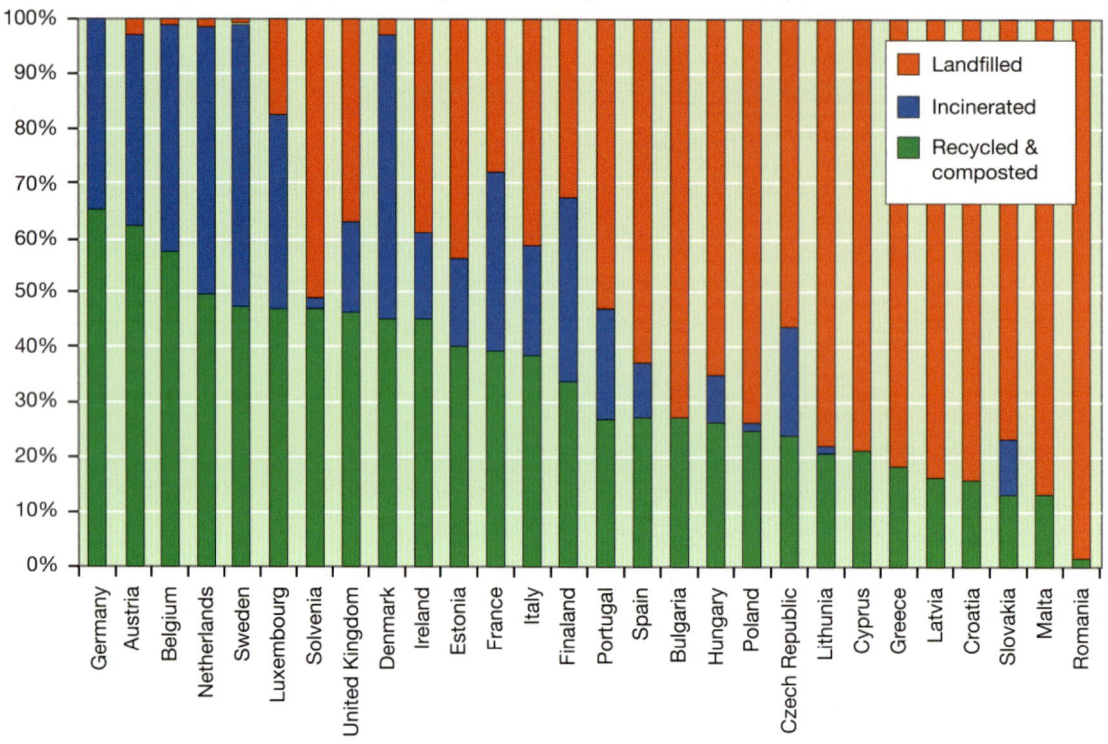

Source: G. Nagle, 2017, Geography IB Course Companion, Oxford

Figure 4.8: A divergent bar graph to show how human activities may lead to global warming and/or global cooling

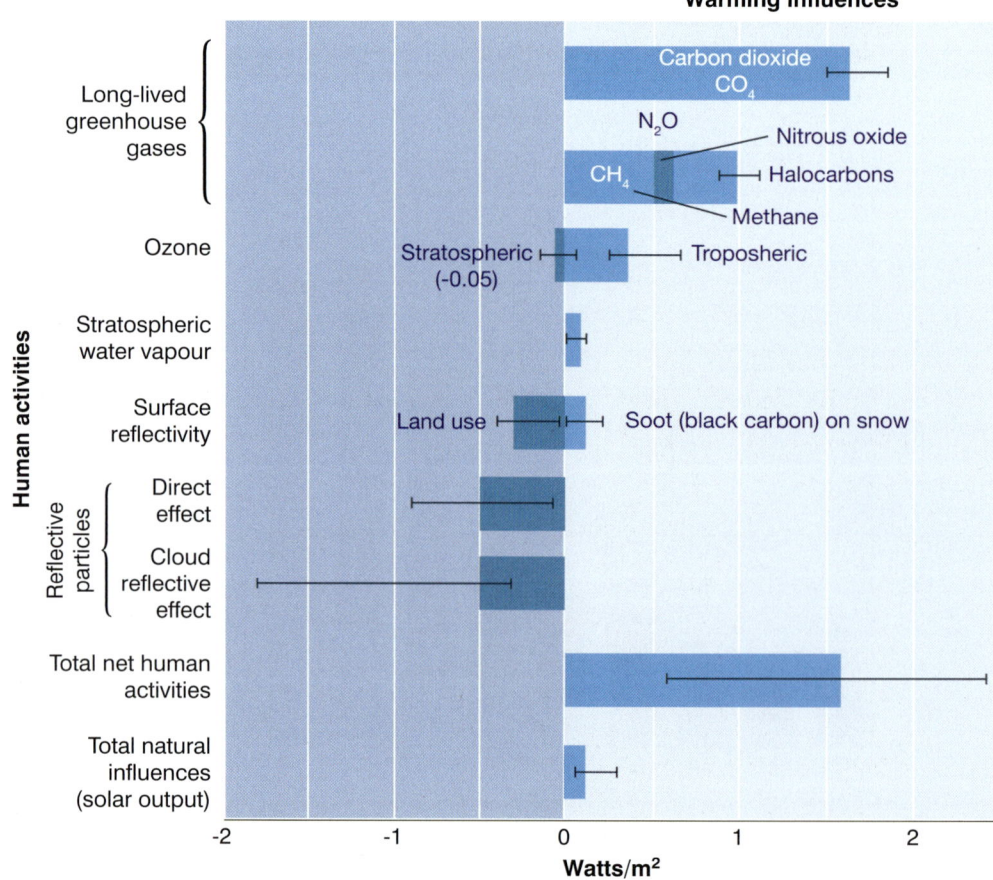

Source: G. Nagle and P. Guinness, 2016, Geography workbook for Cambridge International AS and A level, Hodder

Activities 4.1

Global population	2005	2025
Rural	51%	43%
Urban	49%	57%

Draw a bar graph to illustrate the data in the table above.

Pie charts

Pie charts and **proportional pie charts** are frequently used on maps to show variations in size and composition of a geographical feature. Every 3.6° on the pie chart represents 1%, thus the 360° of the circle represents 100%. To plot values, first convert them to percentages and then multiply by 3.6. This gives the number of degrees that each segment will be. For example, the percentage contribution of deaths in children under 5 years is shown below.

Diarrhoea	15	HIV/AIDS/Measles	3
Prematurity	12	Other	34
Malaria	9	Pneumonia	18
Birth asphyxia	9		

Figure 4.9: Global deaths in children under 5 years by cause (% of total)

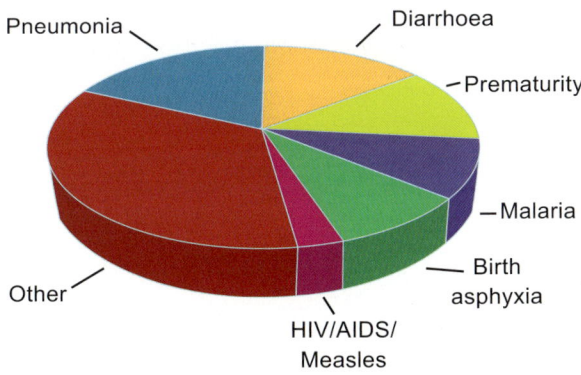

Activities 4.2
Draw a pie chart to show the contributions of different sectors to the ecological footprint of the average London resident.

Sector	Contribution to ecological footprint (%)
Housing and energy	24
Transport	17
Food	26
Consumer goods	13
Private services	7
Government and other	11
Capital investment	2

Using proportional circles

The size (area) of the circle has to be proportional to the value it represents. The area of a circle is found by using the formula πr^2, therefore the circles are drawn in relation to the square root of the value. Decide on the size of the largest circle to be used. Write down its radius (r). Work out the square root of all the values to be mapped. Using the square root of the largest value to be mapped, work out the value (v) that it must be multiplied by in order to make the actual circle on the map. Then multiply all the other square roots by the value (v).

The advantages of pie carts and proportional pie charts are that they are very clear, can show a large amount of data, and can be very striking. The main disadvantage – especially of proportional pie charts – is that they over-emphasise large values, and so small values are not as clear. They also require time, care and patience to draw.

Activities 4.3

Population of large cities

Size of city (million inhabitants)	2005	2025
0.5-1.0	313	390
> 1.0-5.0	711	1,057
> 5.0-10.0	217	337
> 10.0	268	447

Use proportional circles to show the data in the table above.

Scatter graphs

Figure 4.10: A scatter-graph to show the relationship between PPP and IMR

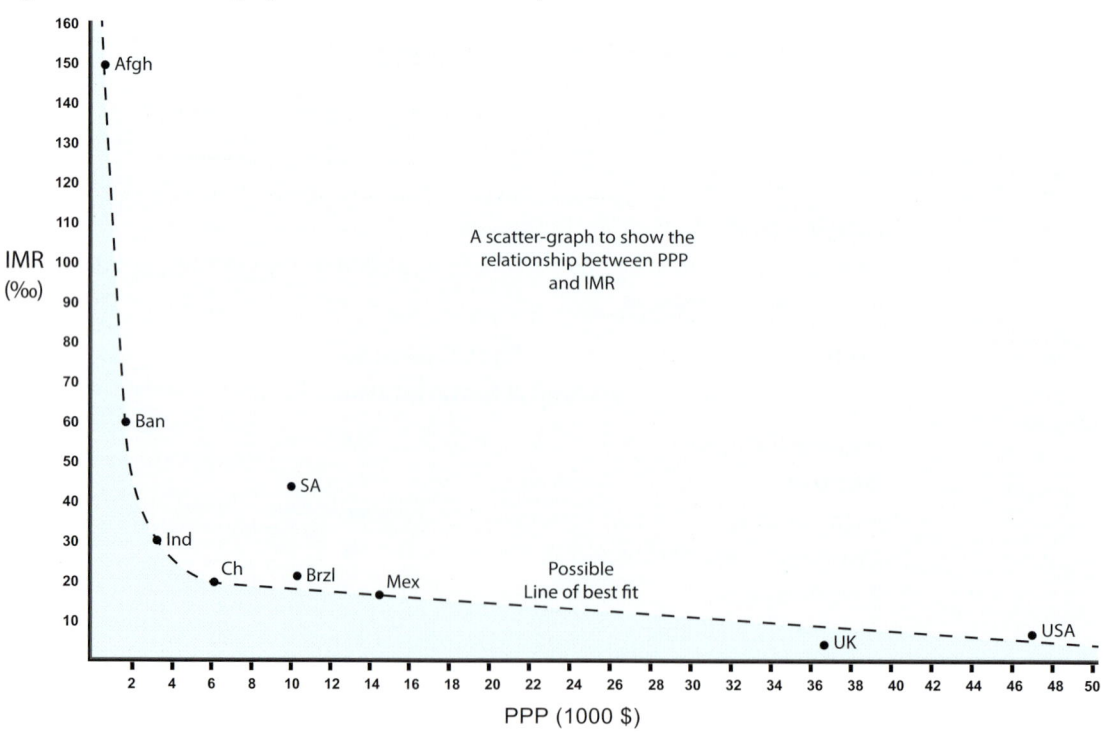

Scatter graphs show how two sets of data are related to each other, for example, purchasing power parity (PPP) and number of Infant Mortality Rate (IMR) or distance from the source of a river and average pebble size. To plot a scatter graph decide which variable is independent (in this example PPP) and which is dependent (IMR). The independent is plotted on the horizontal or X Axis and the dependent on the vertical or Y Axis. For each set of data project a line from the corresponding X and Y Axis where the two lines meet a dot or an x is marked.

Activities 4.4

Construct a scatter graph using the following data.

Site	Discharge (m³/sec)	Suspended load (g/m³)
1	0.45	10.8
2	0.42	9.7
3	0.51	11.2
4	0.55	11.3
5	0.68	12.5
6	0.75	12.8
7	0.89	13.0
8	0.76	12.7
9	0.96	13.0
10	1.26	17.4

When all the data are plotted a line of best fit is drawn. This does not have to pass through the origin. It is useful to label some of the points, for example the highest, smallest anomalies (exceptions), especially if these are referred to in any later description.

Triangular graphs

Triangular graphs are used to show data that can be divided into three parts, e.g. soil (sand, silt and clay), employment (primary, secondary and tertiary), and population (young, adult and elderly) (Figure 4.11). It requires the data are in the form of a percentage and that the percentage totals 100%. The main advantages of triangular graphs is that they allow:

- a large number of data to be shown on one graph (think how many pie charts or bar charts would be used to show all the data on Figure 4.11);
- groupings are easily recognisable. In the case of soils, groups of soil texture can be identified;
- dominant characteristics can be shown easily;
- classifications can be drawn up.

They can be tricky and it is easy to get confused especially if care is not taken, however they provide a fast reliable way of classifying large amounts of data which have three components.

Figure 4.11: Triangular graphs

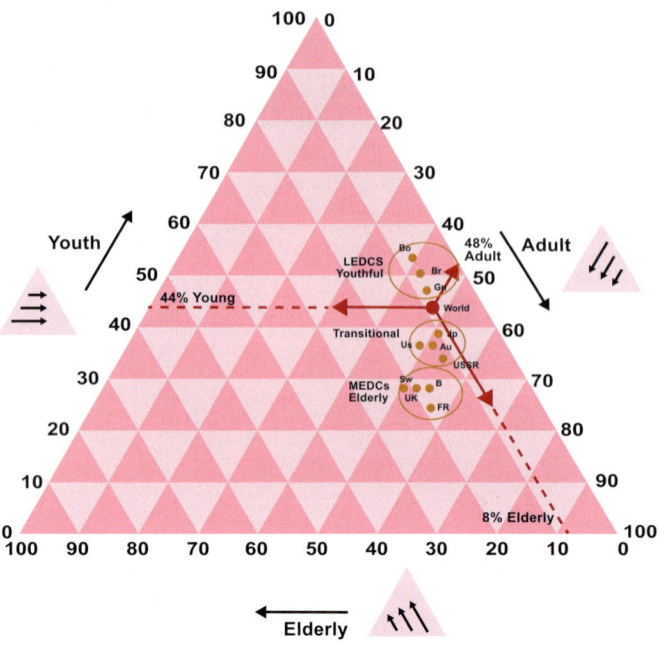

Activities 4.5

On a copy of the triangular graph below show how the workforce of Korea has changed over time.

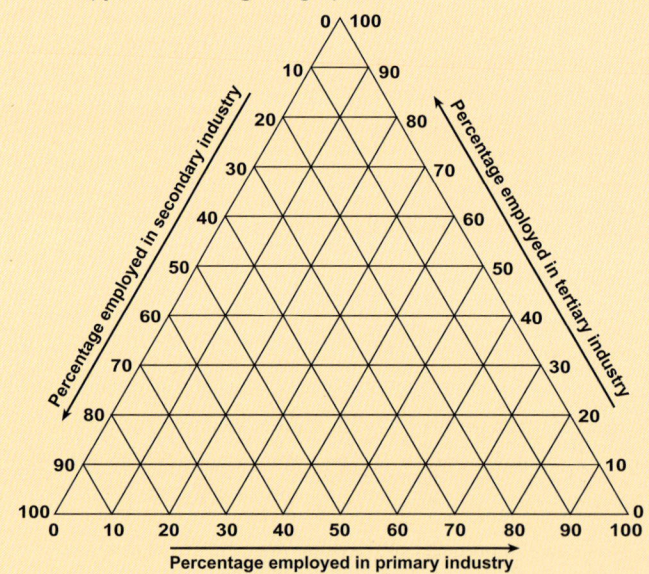

	Primary industries	Secondary industries	Tertiary industries
1970	50.4	14.3	35.3
1980	34.0	22.5	43.5
1990	17.9	27.6	54.5
2000	10.9	20.2	68.9

Dispersion diagrams

A dispersion diagram is a very useful diagram for showing the range of a set of data, their tendency to group or disperse, and also for comparing two groups of data. It involves plotting the values of a single variable on a vertical axis. Technically, there is a short horizontal axis showing frequency. What is revealed is the frequency distribution. Dispersion diagrams can be used to determine the class intervals for choropleth maps.

A critical part of analysing any array of values by means of the dispersion diagram is to determine the median, upper and lower quartile values and therefore the interquartile range.

Figure 4.12: A dispersion diagram to show lichen growth on sides of a gravestone

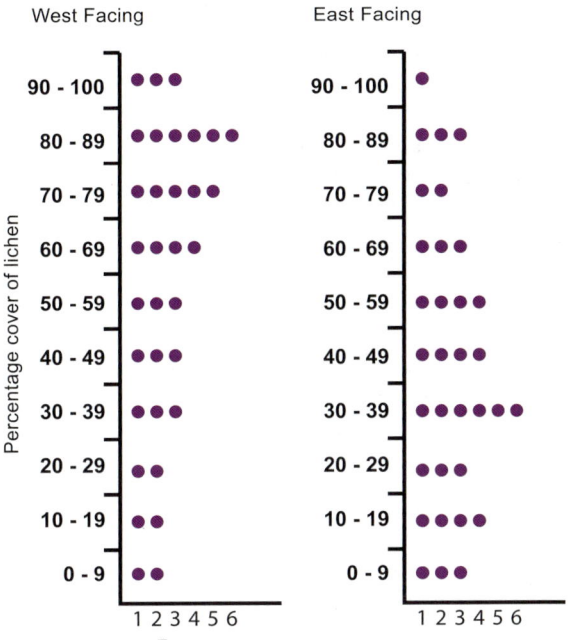

Polar graphs and rose diagrams

Figure 4.13a: Polar graph showing cirque orientation in upland area

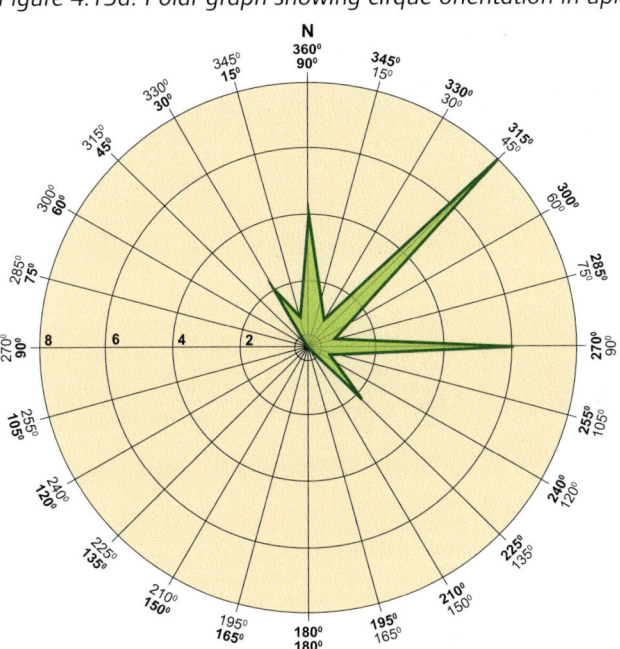

A polar graph is used to show direction as well as magnitude whereas a rose diagram is used to show the composition of a feature. Figure 4.13a shows the direction that glacial cirques in an upland area face. It is quite clear from the diagram that most face either northwards or eastwards. Figure 4.13b shows the orientation of the long axes of pebbles in glacial deposits – the dominant movement is north-west to south-east.

Figure 4.13b: Polar graph showing pebble orientation

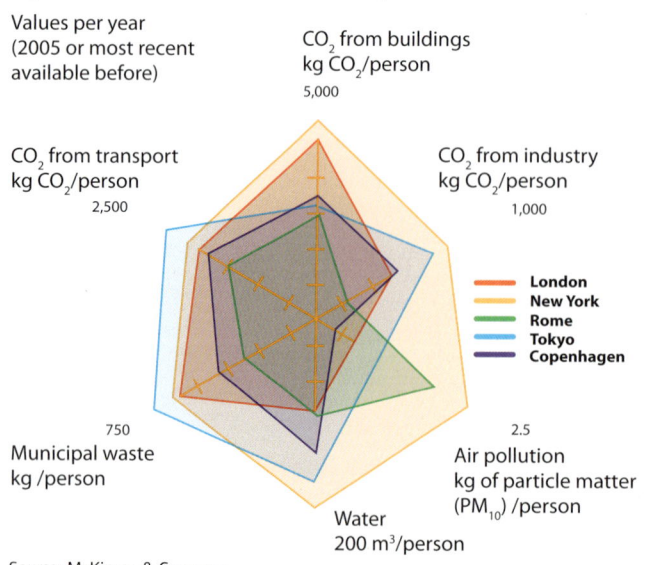

The method for constructing a polar graph is quite simple. Using a compass and a protractor, lines are drawn that correspond with north (0), north-east (45), east (90), south-east (135), south (180), south-west (225), west (270) and north-west (315).

For a rose diagram, the compass points (or other fractions such as sixths – as in Figure 4.14) become different component parts of a whole – for example, the environmental footprint of different cities (Figure 4.14).

Figure 4.14: The environmental footprint for selected cities

Values per year
(2005 or most recent available before)

CO_2 from buildings
kg CO_2/person
5,000

CO_2 from transport
kg CO_2/person
2,500

CO_2 from industry
kg CO_2/person
1,000

London
New York
Rome
Tokyo
Copenhagen

750
Municipal waste
kg /person

2.5
Air pollution
kg of particle matter
(PM_{10}) /person

Water
200 m³/person

Source: McKinsey & Company

Kite diagrams

A kite diagram is a form of line graph where the scale is split in two i.e. half the value is shown above a horizontal line and half below. They are most commonly used to show vegetation distribution, as for example, across a sand dune system. The section for the sand-dune profile is an example of a cross section.

Figure 4.15: Kite diagram to show vegetation density on Studland sand dunes

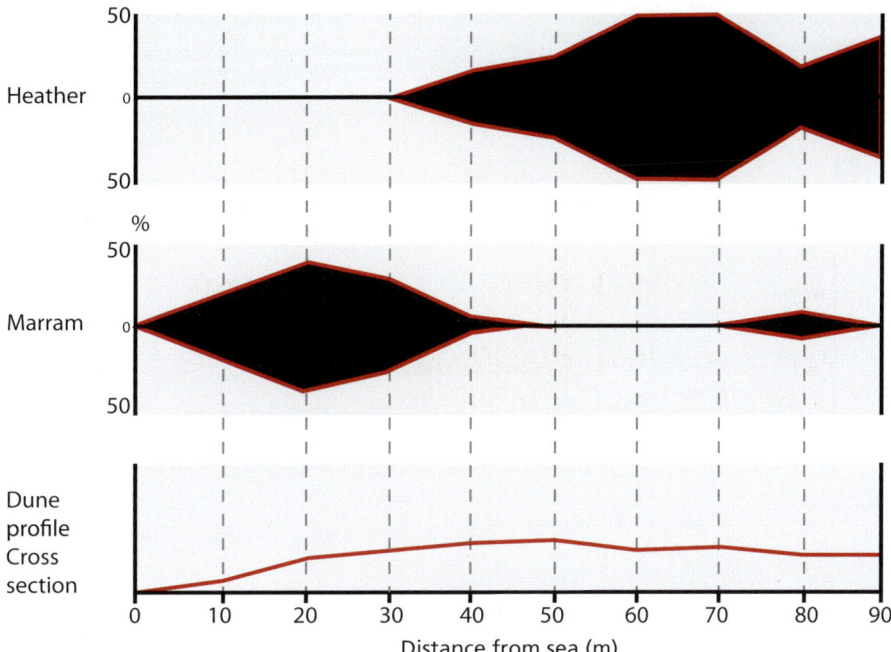

Semi-log and double-log (log-log) graphs

Semi-logarithmic graph paper has a 'normal' scale on one axis – usually the horizontal or y-axis – and a logarithmic scale on the other (Figure 4.16). Semi-log graphs are used to show data that have a particularly wide range of values.

Figure 4.16: Semi-log graph to show population growth in selected settlements, 1801-1901

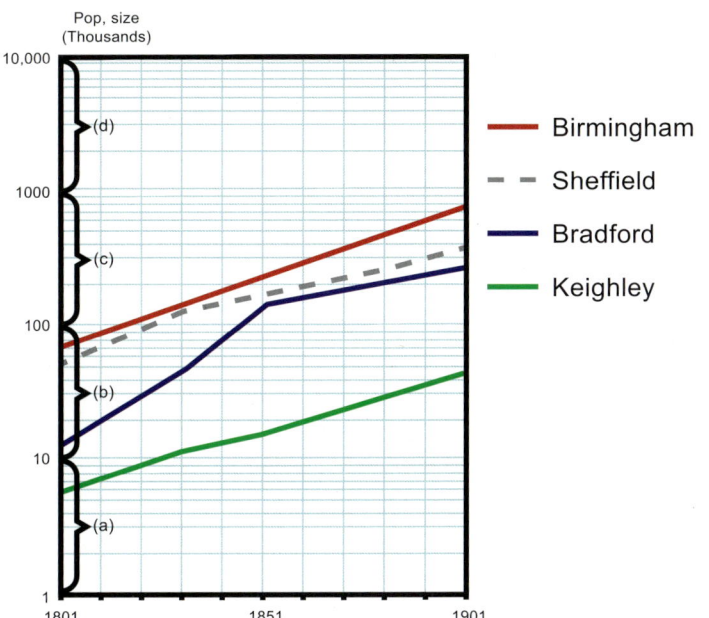

The logarithmic scale compresses the range of values. It gives more space to the smaller values and reduces the amount of space for the larger values. Thus, it can show relative growth quite clearly. On the scale there are 'cycles' of values, shown by the letters 'a' to 'd'. Each cycle increases by a larger amount, usually to the power of 10.

In some cases, logarithmic scales can be used on both axes (Figure 4.17). This is known as a double log scale. The Hjulstrom Curve is drawn on a log-log scale. This is used when both sets of data have large ranges. The data for North Oxfordshire settlements and amount of reported crime has very large ranges for both settlement size and for amount of reported crime – hence a double log scale is used.

Figure 4.17: Double log graph to show settlement size and amount of reported crime

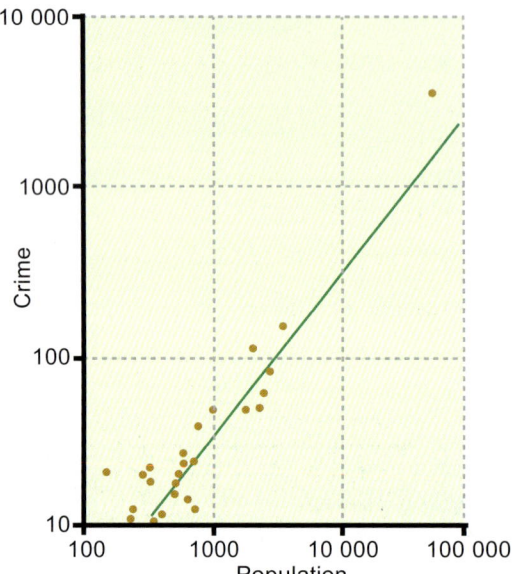

Lorenz curves

The Lorenz Curve and the Gini Coefficient are measures of concentration. The Lorenz Curve is a visual method of showing inequalities whereas the Gini Coefficient provides a statistical measure of inequalities. Typically, Lorenz curves are used to show inequalities in wealth (as in Figure 4.18), which shows inequality in wealth in Rio de Janeiro, and in population density, as in Figure 4.19. Lorenz curves make use of cumulative percentage data, and points are plotted in the order of largest to smallest. The greater the distance from the diagonal line (even distribution), the greater the degree of concentration.

Figure 4.18: Lorenz curve to show inequality in wealth in Rio de Janeiro

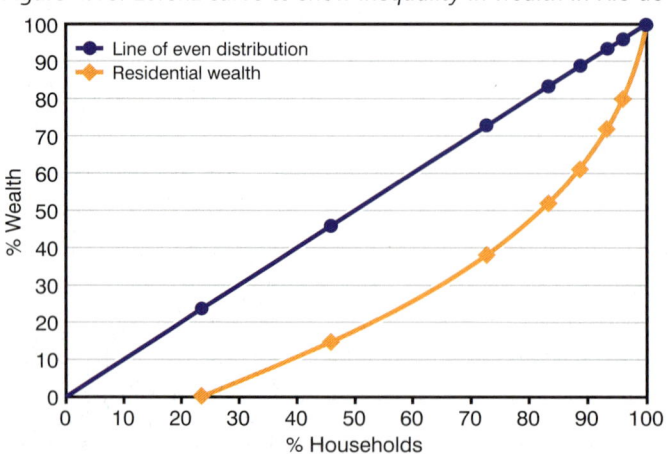

Source: Vetter, D., et al., 2014, Residential wealth distribution in Rio de Janeiro, Land Lines, Lincoln Institute of Land Policy, January 2014, Figure 5, Page 19

Lorenz curve for UK population data

The following data provides data for the UK, 2014.

Table 4.1: Population data for the UK's regions, 2014

Region	Area (sq km)	Population (million)	Population density (population/ sq km)	% of UK's population (rounded to nearest whole number)	% of UK's land
UK	244,111	64.6	265	100	100
North East	15,401	2.6	169	4.0	6.3
North West	7,331	7.1	968	11.0	3.0
Yorks and Humber	15,420	5.4	350	8.3	6.3
East Midlands	15,630	4.6	294	7.1	6.4
West Midlands	13,013	5.7	438	8.8	5.3
East	12,573	6.0	477	9.2	5.1
South East*	27,222	17.4	639	26.9	11.1
South West	23,850	5.4	226	8.3	9.7
Wales	20,768	3.1	149	4.7	8.5
Scotland	78,783	5.3	67	8.2	32.2
Northern Ireland	14,120	1.8	127	2.8	5.7

*Includes London – sometimes London is given as a separate entry – in 2014 London's population was 8.5 million, and its average population density was 5,432 people/sq km.

Table 4.2: Cumulative percentage of population and land, by highest population density*

Cumulative* percentage of population and land, by highest population density	Region	% UK's population	% UK's land	Cumulative % of UK's population	Cumulative % of UK's land
968	North West	11.0	3.0	11.0	3.0
639	South East	26.9	11.1	37.9	14.1
477	East	9.2	5.1	47.1	19.2
438	West Midlands	8.8	5.3	55.9	24.5
350	Yorks and Humber	8.3	6.3	64.2	30.8
294	East Midlands	7.1	6.4	71.3	37.2
226	South West	8.3	9.7	79.6	46.9
169	North East	4.0	6.3	83.6	53.2
149	Wales	4.7	8.5	88.3	61.7
127	Northern Ireland	2.8	5.7	91.1	67.4
67	Scotland	8.2	32.2	99.3	99.6

*Found by adding the top two regions, then the top three most densely population regions and so on

Figure 4.19: Lorenz curve showing inequalities in population density in UK regions

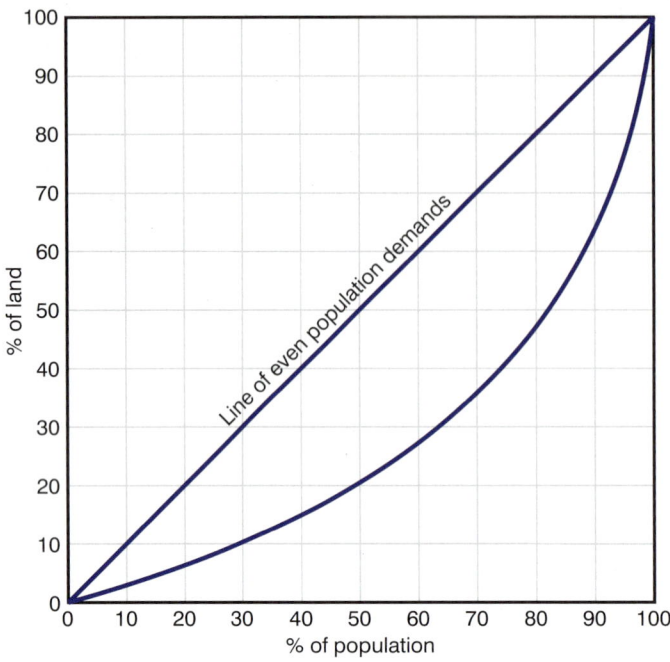

Activities 4.6

The table below shows income inequality in five countries.

Country	Household income of richest 10%	Household income of poorest 10%
South Africa	51.3	1.2
Zambia	47.4	1.5
Brazil	41.6	1.2
China	31.4	2.1
Norway	21.2	3.8

Plot the data for income inequality for the five countries. Also include the line of income equality.

Chapter 5
Statistical skills

Measures of central tendency

There are many types of statistics, some of them extremely easy and some very complex. At the most basic there are simple **descriptive** statistics. These include the **mean** or **average**, the **maximum, minimum range** (maximum-minimum), the **mode** (the most frequently occurring number, group or class) and the **median** (the middle value when all the numbers are placed in ascending or descending rank order).

We have seen that there are four different types of data:

- **Nominal** data refer to objects which have names, such as rock types, land-uses, dates of floods, famines, and so on.

- **Ordinal** (or **ranked**) data are placed in ascending or descending order, for example settlement hierarchies are often expressed in terms of ranks. Spearman's Rank Correlation Coefficient is used to compare two sets of ranked data such as infant mortality rate and gross national income.

- **Interval** or **ratio** data refer to real numbers – **interval data** has no true zero (as in the case of temperature which can be in °C or °F) whereas **ratio data** possess a true zero (as in the case of rainfall).

Summarising data

Table 5.1: CO_2 emissions per capita (mt)

Country	CO_2 emissions per capita (mt)
USA	19.5
China	4.3
Russia	10.5
India	1.3
Japan	9.6
Germany	9.5
Canada	16.1
UK	9.1
South Korea	9.4
Italy	7.7
Mexico	4.1
South Africa	8.7
Indonesia	1.9
France	6.2
Brazil	1.7
Egypt	2.2
Ecuador	2.2
Ukraine	6.9
Australia	18.1
Saudi Arabia	16.5
$\Sigma = 165.5$	

Source World Development Report, 2010, Development and climate change

The **mean** or average is found by totalling (Σ) the values (x) for all observations and then dividing by the total number of observations (n), thus $\Sigma x/n$. In this case the average CO_2 emissions/country is 165.5/20 = 8.275 so we round up to 8.3.

The **mode** refers to the group or class which occurs most often. In this case the mode is 2.2.

Another statistic is the **median**. This is the middle value when all the data are placed in ascending or descending order. In this case, because there are two middle values (the 10th and 11th values) we take the average of these two. In this case they are 7.7 and 8.7, so the median (middle) value is 8.2, which is not a value in the data set.

Summarising groups of data

In some cases the data we collect is in the form of a group e.g. daily rainfall, slope angles or ages may be recorded as 0-4, 5-9, 10-14, 15-19 etc.

The data below shows daily rainfall in an area of rainforest. To make recording simpler groups of 5 mm have been used. Finding an average is slightly more difficult. We use the mid-point of the group and multiply this by the frequency.

Table 5.2: Daily rainfall for an area of tropical rainforest in Brunei

Daily rainfall (mm)	Mid-point	Frequency	Mid point x frequency
0-4	2	20	40
5-9	7	42	294
10-14	12	24	288
15-19	17	12	204
20-24	22	2	44
Total		**n = 100**	**Σx = 870**

Mean = $\Sigma x/n$ = 870/100 = 8.7

The **modal group** is the one which occurs with the most frequency i.e. 5-9 mm. The **median** or middle value will be the average of the 50th and 51st values when ranked: these are both in the 5-9 mm group.

Measures of dispersion

The range is the difference between the **maximum** (largest) and the **minimum** (smallest) value. In the example in Table 5.1 the maximum is 19.5 and the minimum is 1.3, hence the range is 19.5 -1.3, namely 18.2. An alternative measure is the **interquartile range**. This is similar to the range but only gives the range of the middle half of the results – by this the extremes are omitted. The **interquartile** range is found by removing the top and bottom **quartiles** (quarters) and stating the range that remains. The top quartile is found by taking the 25% highest values and finding the mid-point between the top 25% and the next point. The lower quartile is found by taking the 25% lowest values and finding the mid-point between these and the next highest value. The first quartile is termed Q1, and the third quartile Q3.

Hence the interquartile range in the case of CO_2 emissions is mid-way between the 5th and 6th value (i.e. half way between 10.5 and 9.6, namely 10.05) and mid-way between the 15th and 16th values, (i.e. half-way between 4.1 and 2.2, namely 3.15). The result is 10.05 -3.15 which equals 6.9 showing a much smaller variation than when all values (including extremes) were included.

Not every case is as easy! For example, there may be 21, 22 or 23 figures, rather than in this case where the number of observations is divisible by 4. In those situations we have to make an informed guess at where the quartile would be.

If we take the case of 21 observations then the quartiles are at 5¼ and 16¾. In the above example, the figure for Poland is added (7.9 mt) to give a 21st value.

The principle is the same as before. Find the values which represent 25% and 75% of the values. Then, find half the difference between the bottom of the top 25% and the next value below. Then find half the difference between the top of the lowest 25% and the next value above.

The 25% value is found ¼ of the way between 10.5 and 9.6 (i.e. 5¼ along the scale as there are now 21 values), while the 75% value (16¾) lies ¾ of the way between 6.2 and 4.3. Thus the first quartile is found by adding one quarter of the difference of 10.5 and 9.6 from 10.5 i.e.

$$10.5 - \frac{(10.5 - 9.6)}{4} = 10.225 \text{ (rounded to 10.2)}$$

Q1 is mid-way between 10.2 and 9.6, i.e 9.9.

The 75% value is found by taking three quarters of the difference of 6.2 and 4.3 from 6.2 i.e.

$$6.2 - \frac{3(6.2 - 4.3)}{4} = 4.775 \text{ (rounded to 4.8)}$$

Q3 Is located midway between 6.2 and 4.8, namely 5.5.

Thus, the interquartile range is 9.9 – 5.5 i.e. 4.4.

In the next case there are twenty two observations as the data have been extended to include Nigeria at 0.8mt/person.

The 25% and 75% values now are found at 5½ and 16½ (as each quarter is 5½ in size, i.e. 22/4). Thus the 25% is found half way between the 5th and 6th figures, 10.5 and 9.6 (i.e. 10.05 rounded to 10.1) and the 75% is found half way between the 17th and 18th values, 4.3 and 4.1 (i.e. 4.2). Hence Q1 is found half way between the 25% value and the next value below, i.e. midway between 10.1 and 9.6, namely 9.85 rounded to 9.9. Q3 is found half way between the 75% value and the next value above, i.e. the midpoint between 4.2 and 4.3 namely 4.25 rounded up to 4.3.

Thus the interquartile range in this case is 9.9 – 4.3 = 5.6 mt.

Standard deviation

Another way of showing grouping around a central value is by using the standard deviation. This is one of the most important descriptive statistics because

- it takes into account all the values in a distribution; and
- it is necessary for probability and for more complex statistics. It measures dispersal of figures around the mean, and is calculated by first measuring the mean and then comparing the difference of each value from the mean.

It is based on the ideas of probability. If a number of observations are made then we would expect most to be quite close to the average, few very much larger or smaller, and equal proportions that are above and below the mean. In this case, however, there are almost three times as many countries below the average as above it. How does this compare with the value for the average HDI?

The formula for the standard deviation $= \sqrt{\Sigma(x-\bar{x})^2/n}$

where x refers to each observation, $\bar{x}$ to the mean, n the number of points, and $(x-\bar{x})^2$ tells us to take the mean from each observation, and then to square the result. The following example shows the working out.

Table 5.3: Computing the standard deviation

Country	x	$\bar{x}$	$(x-\bar{x})$	$(x-\bar{x})^2$
	CO_2 emissions per capita (mt)			
USA	19.5	8.3	11.2	125.44
China	4.3	8.3	–4	16
Russia	10.5	8.3	2.2	4.84
India	1.3	8.3	–7	49
Japan	9.6	8.3	1.3	1.69
Germany	9.5	8.3	1.2	1.44
Canada	16.1	8.3	7.8	60.84
UK	9.1	8.3	0.8	0.64
South Korea	9.4	8.3	1.1	1.21
Italy	7.7	8.3	–0.6	0.36
Mexico	4.1	8.3	–4.2	17.64
South Africa	8.7	8.3	0.4	0.16
Indonesia	1.9	8.3	–6.4	40.96
France	6.2	8.3	–2.1	4.41
Brazil	1.7	8.3	–6.6	43.56
Egypt	2.2	8.3	–6.1	37.21
Ecuador	2.2	8.3	–6.1	37.21
Ukraine	6.9	8.3	–1.4	1.96
Australia	18.1	8.3	9.8	96.04
Saudi Arabia	16.5	8.3	8.2	67.24
	$\Sigma = 165.5$			$\Sigma = 607.85$

Thus, the standard deviation is found by putting the figures into the formula:

$$(s) = \sqrt{\frac{607.85}{20}} = \sqrt{30.3925} = 5.51, \text{ rounded down to } 5.5$$

Thus, the average deviation of all values around the mean (8.3) is 5.5. This gives a much more accurate figure than the range or the IQR, as it takes into account all values and is not as affected by extreme values. Given normal probability we would expect that c.68% of the observations will fall within 1 standard deviation of the mean, c.95% within 2 standard deviations of the mean, and c.99% within 3 standard deviations (Figure 5.1). Here we can see quite clearly that the rich countries are well above average (and some are over the mean plus two standard deviations, whereas the poorer countries are much more similar in income – they are all within one standard deviation of the mean).

Figure 5.1: Standard deviations and probability

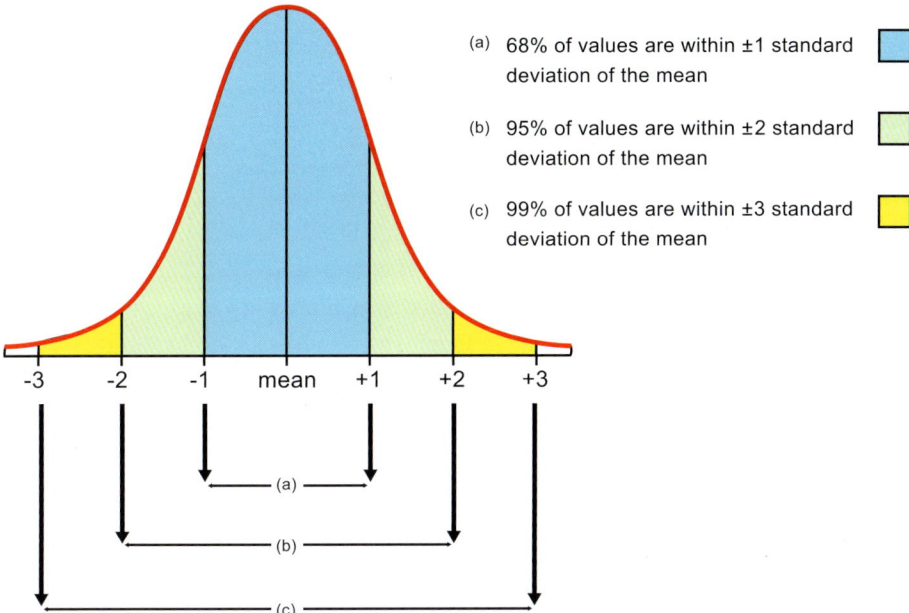

(a) 68% of values are within ±1 standard deviation of the mean

(b) 95% of values are within ±2 standard deviation of the mean

(c) 99% of values are within ±3 standard deviation of the mean

Activities 5.1

The following data show rainfall figures over a 22-year period.

509, 704, 710, 593, 577, 571, 752, 598, 634, 473, 683, 528, 654, 597, 578, 731, 608, 702, 662, 609, 471, 591

(i) State the maximum, minimum and work out the range for the data set.

(ii) Work out the interquartile range.

(iii) Calculate the mean and standard deviation of the data set.

(iv) Why is the mean and standard deviation considered to be a better 'average' than the interquartile range?

(v) Given normal probability, what percentage of the data set ought to lie within one-, two- and three-standard deviations of the mean?

Inferential and relational statistical techniques

Inferential statistics use results from surveys to make estimates or predictions i.e. they make an inference about the total population or about some future situation. To understand inferential statistics it is important to grasp three related concepts, namely probability, significance and sampling.

Probability

One of the main tasks of inferential statistics is to establish the likelihood of a particular event or value occurring – this is known as probability. Probability is measured on a scale from 0 to 1. The value 1 represents absolute certainty (e.g. that everyone will eventually die) whereas the value 0 represents absolute impossibility (that a non-American citizen will become President of the USA).

In statistics, probability (p) is often expressed as a percentage:

- $p = 0.05$ (a 1 in 20 chance) is a 95% level of probability;

- $p = 0.01$ (a one in one hundred chance) is a 99% level of probability;

- $p = 0.001$ (a one in one thousand chance) is a 99.9% level of probability.

Sampling

The key aspect here is to decide how reliable our sample size is and how accurately it allows us to predict i.e. what is the probability that our sample is truly representative.

Significance

Significance relates to the probability that a hypothesis is true. In statistics, it is convention to use a **null hypothesis** (H_0) (a statement that we aim to reject). A null hypothesis might state, for example, that there is no difference in the water quality above and below a sewage outlet. The **alternative hypothesis** (H_1) (also known as the research hypothesis) would state that 'there is a difference between the water quality above and below a sewage outlet'. The probability at which it is decided to reject the null hypothesis is known as the **significance level**. The significance level indicates the number of times that the observed differences could be caused by chance. The practice is to refer to results as 'significant', 'highly significant' and 'very highly significant' respectively when significant at the 95%, 99% and 99.9% levels of significance. This means there is a 1 in 20, 1 in 100 and 1 in 1000 chance (probability) of the result occurring by chance.

Student's t-test

The t-test is often used to test whether two samples are independent of each other, or whether they could be drawn from the same background population. It can also be used to test the significance of Spearman's Rank Correlation Coefficient. It is difficult to work out (but is available on most computing/spreadsheet software) but it is important to know how and why it is used.

T-test for independent samples

The t-test for independent samples is used when the data collection for one sample (x) has no bearing on the selection of the samples for the other category (y). For example, a survey of slope angles in an area of chalk and clay produced the following results:

Chalk slope angles (°): 13, 11, 15, 12, 15, 18, 12, 19, 16, 18

Clay slope angles (°): 6, 2, 8, 7, 3, 9, 6, 1, 5, 7

Table 5.4: Computing the t-test

Chalk (x)	Clay (y)	$x - \bar{x}$	$(x - \bar{x})^2$	$y - \bar{y}$	$(y - \bar{y})^2$
13	6	-1.9	3.61	0.6	0.36
11	2	-3.9	15.21	-3.4	11.56
15	8	0.1	0.01	2.6	6.76
12	7	-2.9	8.41	1.6	2.56
15	3	0.1	0.01	-2.4	5.76
18	9	3.1	9.61	3.6	12.96
12	6	-2.9	8.41	0.6	0.36
19	1	4.1	16.81	-4.4	19.36
16	5	1.1	1.21	-0.4	0.16
18	7	3.1	9.61	1.6	2.56
$\Sigma = 149$, $\bar{x} = 14.9$	$\Sigma = 54$, $\bar{y} = 5.4$		$\Sigma = 72.90$		$\Sigma = 62.6$

Step 1: State the null hypothesis (H_0): there is no difference between the means of the populations x and y.

Step 2: State the alternative hypothesis (H_1): there is a difference between the means of the populations x and y.

Step 3: State the significance level: 95%.

Step 4: Compute Student's t-test.

First, calculate the standard deviations of the populations. As the samples are relatively small in number, a pooled standard deviation is obtained from all the data, using the formula

$$s = \sqrt{(\Sigma (x - \bar{x})^2 + \Sigma (y - \bar{y})^2) / (n_x + n_y - 2)}$$

$$s = \sqrt{((72.9) + (62.6)) / 18} = 2.74$$

Next, calculate the standard deviations of the sampling distributions of $\bar{x}$ and $\bar{y}$ (i.e. the standard error of the sample means)

$$SE_{\bar{x}} = s/\sqrt{n_x} = 2.74/\sqrt{10} = 0.87$$

$$SE_{\bar{y}} = s/\sqrt{n_x} = 2.74/\sqrt{10} = 0.87$$

Thirdly, calculate the standard deviation of the sampling distribution of the difference-between-means (i.e. the standard error of ($\bar{x}$ - $\bar{y}$), using the formula

$$SE_{(\bar{x} - \bar{y})} = \sqrt{((SE_{\bar{x}})^2 + (SE_{\bar{y}})^2)}$$

Therefore, $SE_{(\bar{x} - \bar{y})} = \sqrt{(0.87)^2 + (0.87)^2} = 1.23$

Finally, calculate t:

$$t = \frac{\text{the difference between the means}}{\text{the standard error of the difference}}$$

$$t = \frac{(\bar{x} - \bar{y})}{SE_{(\bar{x} - \bar{y})}} = \frac{14.9 - 5.4}{1.23} = 7.7$$

Thus, at the 95% level of significance, with 18 degrees of freedom, the critical value is 2.1. (The critical value for 99% level of significance is 2.88. Our computed value of 7.7 exceeds the critical values at both the 95% and 99% level of significance, so we can say with 99% certainty, that there is a statistically significant difference between the slope angles associated with chalk and those with clay.)

T-test for paired data

In some cases, the data may be paired or linked. For example, a survey of weathering of gravestones could record data for east and west facing gravestones. Each gravestone has two faces, and so there are paired data for each gravestone.

Table 5.5: Paired data for lichen content on east and west facing gravestones

East-facing	West-facing	Difference (d)	(d - d̄)	(d - d̄)²
58	76	18	0.58	0.34
76	88	12	5.42	29.38
32	36	4	13.42	180.1
8	16	8	9.42	88.74
37	59	22	4.58	20.98
95	95	0	17.42	282.48
0	68	68	50.58	2558.34
52	61	9	8.42	70.9
65	72	7	10.42	108.58
0	46	46	28.58	816.82
100	100	0	17.42	282.48
63	78	15	2.43	5.86
Σ = 586, $\bar{x}$ = 48.83	Σ = 795, $\bar{y}$ = 66.25		$\bar{d}$ = 17.42 ($\bar{x} - \bar{y}$) =17.42	Σ = 4445

Calculate the standard deviation of the difference between x and y

$sd = \sqrt{((\Sigma(d - \bar{d})^2)/n-1)} = \sqrt{(4445/11)} = \sqrt{(404.09} = 20.1$

Next, calculate the standard error of the mean differences

$SE_{\bar{d}} = sd/\sqrt{n} = 20.1/\sqrt{12} = 5.80$

Finally, calculate t:

$$t = \frac{\text{the difference between the means}}{\text{the standard error of the difference}}$$

$$t = \frac{\bar{d}}{SE_{\bar{d}}} = \frac{17.42}{5.8} = 3.0$$

With 11 (n-1) degrees of freedom, at the 95% level of significance, the critical value is 2.2. Our computed value of 3 exceeds this, so we can reject with 95% confidence the null hypothesis, and accept the alternative hypothesis i.e. there is a 95% statistically significant difference between the lichen cover on east- and west-facing gravestones. Interestingly, at the 99% level, the computed value is not statistically significant, as the critical value is 3.11.

Spearman's Rank Correlation Coefficient (Rs)

Spearman's Rank Correlation Coefficient (Rs) is one of the most widely used statistics in social and environmental sciences. It is relatively quick and easy to do and only requires that data are available on the **ordinal (ranked)** scale. More complex data can be transformed into ranks very simply. It is called a 'rank' correlation because only the ranks are correlated not the actual values. The use of Rs allows us to decide whether or not there is a significant **statistical correlation (relationship)** between two sets of data. In some cases it is clear whether a correlation exists or not. However, in most cases it is not so clear cut and to avoid subjective comments we use Rs to bring in a certain amount of objectivity.

Table 5.6: Organic content and moisture content in a sample of soils

Sample	Organic content (O.C.) (%)	Moisture content (M.C.) (%)
1	3.8	15
2	4.7	22
3	6.2	30
4	3.9	18
5	5.4	24
6	7.1	29
7	6.2	26
8	4.6	20
9	4.6	25
10	5.1	20

Procedure

1. State the **null hypothesis** (H_0) that there is no significant relationship between organic content (OC) and moisture content (MC). The alternative hypothesis (H_1) is that there is a significant relationship between the two variables.

2. Rank both sets of data from high to low i.e. highest value gets rank 1, second highest 2, and so on. In the case of joint ranks find the average rank e.g. if two values occupy positions two and three they both take on rank 2.5, if three values occupy positions four, five and six, they all take rank 5.

3. Using the formula

$$Rs = 1 - \frac{6\Sigma d^2}{n^3 - n}$$

work out the correlation, where 'd' refers to the difference between ranks and 'n' the number of observations.

4. Compare the computed Rs with the critical values in the statistical tables.

Table 5.7: Worked example of Spearman's Rank Correlation Coefficient

Sample	% O.C.	% M.C.	Rank O.C.	Rank M.C.	Difference in ranks (d)	d^2
1	3.8	15	10	10	0	0
2	4.7	22	6	6	0	0
3	6.2	30	2.5	1	1.5	2.25
4	3.9	18	9	9	0	0
5	5.4	24	4	5	-1	1
6	7.1	29	1	2	-1	1
7	6.2	26	2.5	3	-0.5	0.25
8	4.6	20	7.5	7.5	0	0
9	4.6	25	7.5	4	3.5	12.25
10	5.1	20	5	7.5	-2.5	6.25
						$\Sigma d^2 = 23$

$$Rs = 1 - \frac{6\Sigma d^2}{n^3 - n} = 1 - \frac{6 \times 23}{1000 - 10} = 1 - \frac{138}{990} = 1 - 0.14 = 0.86$$

Once we have the computed value we compare it to the critical values. For a sample of 10 these values are 0.564 for 95% significance and 0.746 for 99% significance. The null hypothesis can be rejected at the 95% level of significance. In this example it is clear that the relationship is very strong i.e. there is more than 99% chance that there is a relationship between the data. The next stage would be to offer explanations for the relationship.

It is important to realise that Spearman's has a number of weaknesses which must be borne in mind. First, it requires a sample of not less than seven observations. Second, it tests for linear relationships and would give an answer of 0 for data such as river discharge and frequency, which follows a curvilinear pattern, with few very low or very high flows and a large number of medium flows. Third, it is easy to make meaningless correlations, as between the success of English cricket teams and Infant Mortality Rate in India. Fourth, the question of scale is always important. A survey of river sediment rates and discharge for the whole of a drainage system may give a strong correlation whereas analysis of just the upper catchments gives a much lower result.

As always, statistics are tools to be used. They are only part of the analysis, and we must be aware of their limits.

There are other correlation coefficients – Pearson Product Moment Correlation Coefficient is a more powerful correlation but it requires more sophisticated data. However, it is available on many computer packages. The principles are the same as for Spearman's rank but the data need to be interval or ratio (real numbers) rather than just ranked data, and the correlation tests for a linear relationship.

Testing for significance using the t-test

The Student's T-test can also be used to test the significance of Spearman's Rank Correlation. The formula is:

$$t = \frac{r_s \times \sqrt{(n-2)}}{(1 - r_s^2)}$$

Where r_s = Spearman's Rank correlation coefficient

n = sample size and

t = Student's t-statistic

The calculated value of t is compared with the critical values in the Student's t-tables at the 95% level of significance level and at (n-2) degrees of freedom. By substituting the calculated value of Spearman's Rank, we get

$t = 0.87 \times \sqrt{((10-2)/(1-(0.87)^2)}$

$t = 0.87 \times \sqrt{(8/(1-0.76))}$

$t = 0.87 \times \sqrt{(8/0.24)} = 5.02$

At the 95% level of significance, with 8 (10-2) degrees of freedom, the critical value is 2.31 (and at the 99% level of significance the critical value is 3.36). Thus, we can reject the null hypothesis, with 95% (and/or 99%) level of significance, and accept the alternative hypothesis i.e. there is a statistically significant relationship between soil organic content and moisture content.

Activities 5.2

The data in Table 5.8 gives values for selected countries' GNI per capita (gross national income, $) and life expectancy in years. Using the data (i) state the null hypothesis (ii) find out if there is a correlation between the data, (iii) what form it is (negative or positive) and (iv) how significant the relationship is and whether the null hypothesis can be rejected or not.

Table 5.8: Gross national income (GNI per capita) and life expectancy for selected countries

Country	GNI per capita ($)	Life expectancy
Luxemburg	70,529	79.03
Norway	46,154	79.67
Finland	33,674	78.66
Bahrain	25,431	79.78
Estonia	20,404	72.30
Saudi Arabia	13,267	75.88
Malaysia	12,642	76.96
Uruguay	10,847	75.95
Mexico	10,570	75.63
Turkey	8,932	72.88
Dominican Republic	8,231	73.07
China	7,693	72.88
El Salvador	4,847	71.78
Jamaica	4,611	73.12
Morocco	4,517	71.22
India	3,678	68.59
Ghana	2,616	59.12
Zimbabwe	2,059	38.50
Ethiopia	978	49.23
Madagascar	887	62.14

Source: CIA World Factbook

The Chi-squared test (X^2)

The Chi-squared test is used to test whether there is a significant difference between data. For example, we can use it to test whether there is any difference between altitude and the number of cirques or orientation and the number of cirques. It is also widely used in human geography. A common test is to see whether there are significant differences in levels of well-being between areas.

The Chi-squared test can only be used on data which has the following characteristics.

1. The data must be in the form of frequencies counted in a number of groups.

2. Data must be on the interval or ratio scale (that is it has a precise numerical value) and can be grouped into categories.

3. The total number of observations must be greater than twenty.

4. The expected frequency in any one category must be greater than 5.

Method

1. State the hypothesis being tested – there is a significant difference between two or more sample groups. It is convention to give a null hypothesis, (a negative test) that is that there is no significant difference between the samples.

2. Tabulate the data as shown in the example below. The data being tested for significance is known as the 'observed' frequency, and the column is headed 'O'.

3. Calculate the 'expected' number of frequencies that you would expect to find. These go in column 'E'.

4. Calculate the Chi-squared statistic using the formula: $X^2 = \Sigma(O-E)^2/E$

   where X^2 is the Chi-squared statistic

   Σ is the sum of

   O refers to the observed frequencies, and

   E are the expected frequencies.

5. Calculate the degrees of freedom. This is quite simply one less than the total number of observations (N) i.e. N-1.

6. Compare the calculated figure with the critical values in the significance tables using the appropriate degrees of freedom. Read off the probability that the data frequencies you are testing could have occurred by chance.

Example

The following figures provide data on the number of cirques and their orientation. What is the probability that the number of cirques is related to orientation?

Orientation	Number of cirques
North-east	40
South-east	15
South-west	5
North-west	12

1. The null hypothesis H_0 states: there is **no significant variation** in the frequency of cirques with orientation.

   The alternative hypothesis (H_1) states that there is a **significant difference** in the frequency of cirques and orientation.

2. If there is no difference in the frequency of cirques they should all have roughly the same frequency. That means they will all have about the average. The expected frequency is thus the same as the average frequency which is $(40 + 15 + 5 + 12)/4 = 72/4 = 18$

3.

Orientation	O (Number of cirques)	E (Average)	(O-E)	$(O-E)^2$	$(O-E)^2/E$
North-east	40	18	22	484	26.89
South-east	15	18	3	9	0.5
South-west	5	18	13	169	9.39
North-west	12	18	6	36	2
					$\Sigma = 38.78$

4. Degrees of freedom (df) = (N-1) = (4-1) = 3

5. The critical values for 3 df are:

0.05	0.01
7.82	11.34

Clearly the computed value of 38.78 exceeds the critical values even at the 0.01 level of significance. This means that there is less than one in a hundred (0.01) chance that given the figures above there is no variation in the frequency of cirques and orientation. Therefore we would reject the null hypothesis and accept the alternative hypothesis. This means that there is a significant difference in the frequency of cirques and their orientation.

N.B. The next stage is to offer explanations for the results. Remember the statistic is only used as a means of clarification: it is not an end in itself but a means to help you to explain.

Chi-squared testing when there are more than two samples

It is usual that you may be looking at data which fall into a number of categories rather than the simple case as shown above. The formula is the same, but the means of obtaining the expected values and the degrees of freedom is different. The following example illustrates these points.

The following figures provide data on the destination of migrants in the UK and the reasons for migration.

Table 5.9: Reasons for migration

Observed frequencies (o) Reasons for migration

	Employment	Housing	Other	Total (r)
London	48	50	60	158
Rest of the UK	372	118	352	842
Total (k)	420	168	412	1000

1. The null hypothesis H_0 states: there is no significant variation in the reasons for migration and destination.

   The alternative hypothesis (H_1) states that there is a significant difference in the reasons for migration and destination.

2. If there is no difference in the reasons for migration and destination they should all have roughly the proportion based on the number of migrants into each area. That means they will all have about the average. The expected frequency is found by using the formula

   Σ (r) Σ (k)/N

   for each observation where Σ (r) is the sum of the row, Σ (k) the sum of the column and N the total number of observations. Thus, the expected values (E) for reasons for migration are:

	Employment	Housing	Other	Total (r)
London	158 x 420/1000 = 66	158 x 168/1000 = 27	158 x 412/1000 = 65	158
Rest of the UK	842 x 420/1000 = 354	842 x 168/1000 = 141	842 x 412/1000 = 347	842
Total (k)	420	168	412	1000

And so, we can work out the X^2 statistic,

	Obs (O)	Exp (E)	(O-E)	(O-E)^2	(O-E)^2/E
Lon/Emp	48	66	18	324	5
Lon/Hous	50	27	23	529	19.6
Lon/Other	60	65	5	25	0.4
Rest/Empl	372	354	18	324	0.9
Rest/Housing	118	141	23	529	3.75
Rest/Other	352	347	5	25	0.07
					Σ = 29.72

3. Degrees of freedom (df) = (r-1) (k-1) = (2 x 1) = 2

4. The critical values for 2 df are:

0.05   0.01
5.99   9.4

Clearly the computed value of 29.72 is greater than the critical value at the 0.05 (95%) level of significance, and even that at the 0.01 (99%) level of significance.

Therefore, we would reject the null hypothesis and accept the alternative hypothesis. This means that there is a **significant difference** in the motives for migration and destination.

N.B. The next stage is to offer explanations for the results. Remember the statistic is only used as a means of clarification: it is not an end in itself but a means to help you to explain.

Activities 5.3

1. In a study of a glaciated highland area, a survey found that
   - 10% of the land was above 1100m
   - 20% of the land was between 900m and 1100m
   - 30% of the land was between 700m and 899m
   - 40% of the land was between 500m and 699m

   If there is no variation in the frequency of cirques and altitude we would expect 10% of cirques to be found above 1100m, 20% between 900m and 1100m, 30% between 700m and 899m and 40% between 500m and 699m. In a survey the following results were found:

Altitude	Number of cirques
>1100m	36
900-1100m	18
700-899m	11
500-699m	5
Total	**70**

   The total number observed at each level is the Observed (O). The expected will be 10% of the observed for the >1100m group, 20% of the total for the 900-1100m group, 30% of the total for the 700-899m group and 40% for the 500-699m group.

   What is the probability that there is a relationship between the number of cirques and altitude?

   (i)   State the null hypothesis.
   (ii) Work out the expected frequency for each altitude group.
   (iii) Work out the X^2 statistic.
   (iv) How significant is this?
   (v) Accept or reject the null hypothesis.

2. A survey of bedrock and soil types gave the following results (Table 5.10).

   Table 5.10: Bedrock and soil types

	Podzol	Brown earth	Gley	Total
Sandstone	31	19	8	58
Shale	13	11	18	42
Total	44	30	26	100

   (i)   State the null hypothesis.
   (ii) Work out the expected frequencies.
   (iii) Work out the X^2 statistic.
   (iv) How significant is your answer?
   (v) Accept/reject the null hypothesis.

The Nearest Neighbour Index (NNI)

Part of the study of ecosystems (and vegetation) is concerned with distributions in space and over time. The **spatial distribution** of vegetation in an area can be described by looking at a map. This may lead us to conclude that some types of vegetation (or ecosystems) are scattered, dispersed or concentrated. However, the main weakness with the visual method is that it is **subjective** and individuals differ in their interpretation of the pattern. Some **objective** measure is required and this is provided by the NNI.

There are three main types of pattern which can be distinguished: **uniform or regular**, **clustered or aggregated**, and **random**. These are shown on Figure 5.2. The points may represent individual trees etc. If the pattern is regular the distance between any one point and its nearest neighbour should be approximately the same as from any other point. If the pattern is clustered then many points will be found a short distance from each other and there will be large areas of the map without any points. A random distribution normally has a mixture of some clustering and some regularity.

Figure 5.2: Some Nearest Neighbour patterns

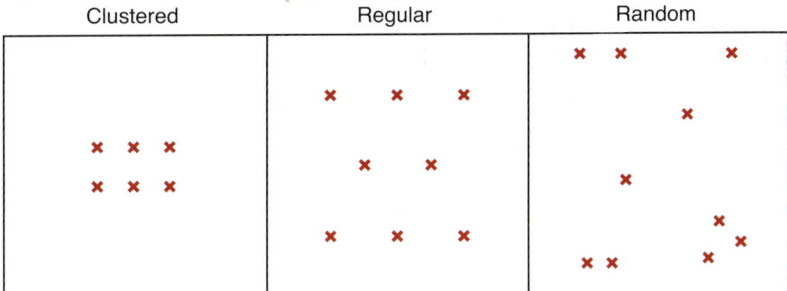

The technique most commonly used to analyse these patterns is the Nearest Neighbour Index (NNI). It is a measure of the spatial distribution of points, and is derived from the average distance between each point and its nearest neighbour. This figure is then compared to computed values which state whether the pattern is regular (NNI = 2.15), clustered (NNI = 0) or random (NNI = 1.0). Thus a value below 1.0 shows a tendency towards clustering, a value of above 1.0 a tendency towards uniformity.

The formula for the NNI looks somewhat daunting at first, but, like most statistics, is extremely straightforward providing care is taken.

NNI or $Rn = 2\bar{D}\sqrt{(N/A)}$

where $\bar{D}$ is the average distance between each point and its nearest neighbour and is calculated by finding $\Sigma d/N$ (d refers to each individual distance), N the number of points under study and A the size of the area under study. It is important that you use the same units for distance and area e.g. metres or km but not a mixture.

For example, a survey of the location of banks and charity stores was carried out in a suburban location (Figure 5.3).

Figure 5.3: The location of banks and charity stores in a suburban location

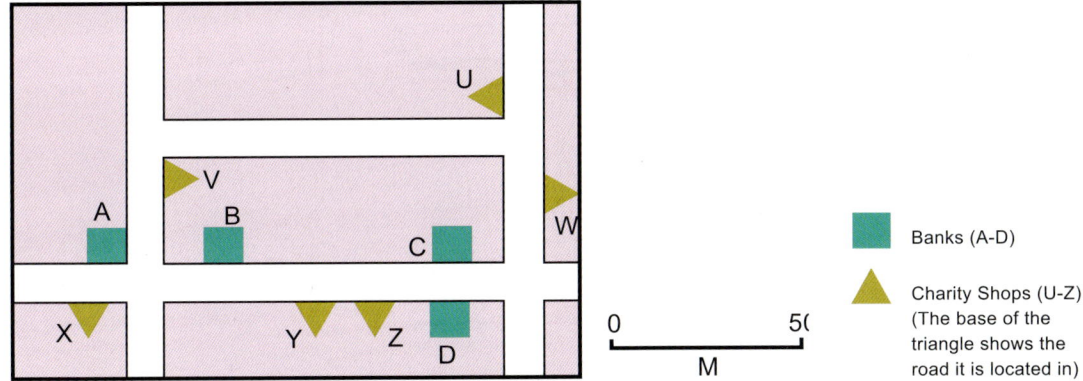

Worked example of Nearest Neighbour statistic

Banks	Nearest neighbour	Distance (m)
A	B	30
B	A	30
C	D	20
D	C	20
		Σd = 100

NNI or Rn = 2D̄ √(N/A)

D̄ = Σd/N = 100/4 = 25

Rn = 2 x 25 x √(4/15,000)

Rn = 0.82

which suggests a slight degree of clustering.

Worked example for charity shops

	Neighest neighbour	Distance (m)
U	X	50
V	W	25
W	V	25
X	U	50
Y	Z	15
Z	Y	15
		Σd = 180

NNI or Rn = 2D̄ √(N/A)

D̄ = Σd/N = 180/6 = 30

Rn = 2 x 30 x √(6/15,000)

Rn = 1.2

which suggests a random pattern with very slight degree of regularity. In neither case is the result significantly clustered (below the lines) or regular (above the lines) (Figure 5.4).

Figure 5.4: Significance levels for nearest neighbour

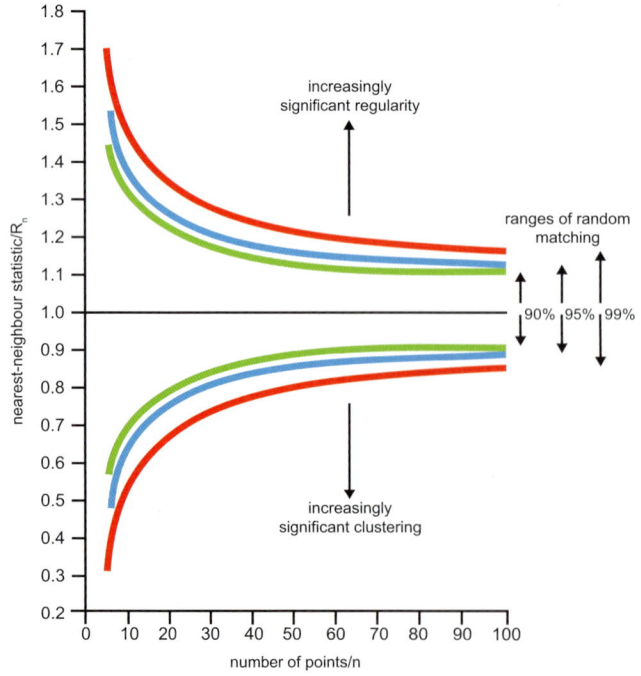

There are important points to bear in mind when using it.

- Two or more sub-patterns (one clustered, one regular) may suggest a random result.

- What is the definition of, for example, a tree? Do you include all individuals – or just those above a certain size?

- Why do we take the nearest neighbour? Why not the third or fourth nearest?

- The choice of the area, and the size of the area studied, can completely alter the result and make a clustered pattern appear regular and vice-versa.

- Although the NNI may suggest a random pattern it may be that the controlling factor e.g. soil type or altitude, is itself randomly distributed, and that the vegetation are in fact located in anything but a random fashion.

> **Activities 5.4**
>
> A survey of the distribution of vegetation types in the Camley Street Natural Park in London was undertaken to plot the distribution of deciduous trees and marsh species. The results have been plotted in Figure 5.5. The area of the nature reserve is approximately 13,200m².
>
> Work out the nearest neighbour statistic for marsh vegetation and for woodland.

Figure 5.5: Location of vegetation types in Camley Street Reserve

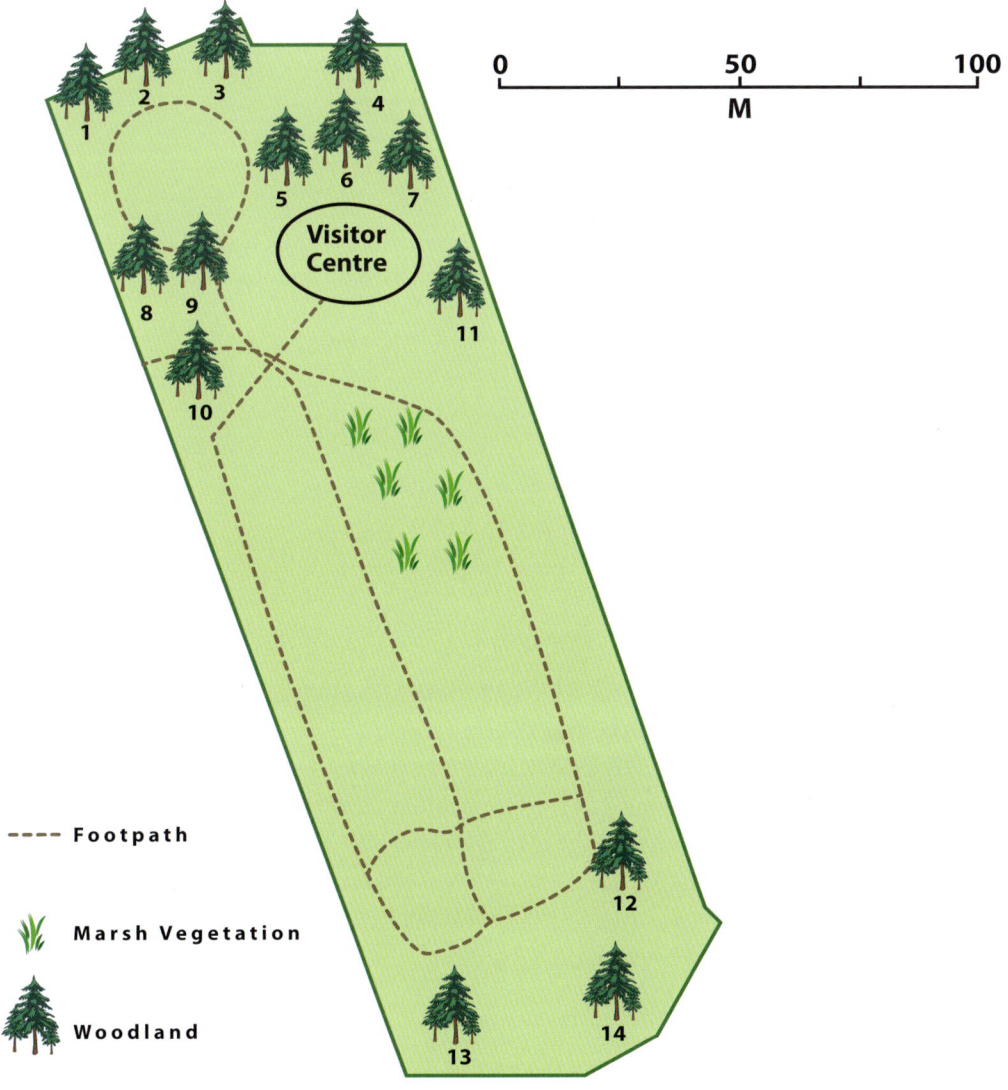

The Mann-Whitney U-Test

This is one of the most powerful distribution (non-parametric) free tests. Even when only medium-sized samples (i.e. 10-20) are involved it has about 95% of the power of Student's T-Test. It can be used with ordinal (ranked) data, as long as both sets are ranked in a single sequence, or with data on an interval scale that have been allotted ranks in a single sequence. It is used to test whether the mean of two independent samples is statistically different i.e. that the samples come from different populations. The samples do not have to be the same size – when the samples are of different sizes the smaller of the two is termed n_1.

Procedure

Water temperature upstream and downstream of a sewage outlet (°C)

Upstream 18, 17, 18, 21, 19

Downstream 23, 24, 21, 20, 22, 23, 24, 22, 23

1. The null hypothesis, H_0, states that is no difference in the means of the two samples. It assumes that the differences between them are the result of 'chance' and are not significant.

2. The alternative hypothesis, H_1, is that there is a significant difference between the two samples, in this case that water temperature below the sewage outlet is significantly higher than above the outlet.

3. The critical level is 95%.

4. To apply the statistic the values must be placed in rank order, but kept in their groups. (Conventionally, the smallest value is given rank 1. Where values tie, assign an average rank to each value.)

   Upstream 2.5, 1, 2.5, 6.5, 4

   Downstream 11, 13.5, 6.5, 5, 8.5, 11, 13.5, 8.5, 11

   The Mann Whitney formula is

   $U = n_1 n_2 + \frac{1}{2} n_1 (n_1 + 1) - R_1$

   Or $U = n_1 n_2 + \frac{1}{2} n_2 (n_2 + 1) - R_2$

   Where R_1 = the sum of the ranks given to values in n_1, and R_2 = the sum of the ranks given to the values in n_2.

   Thus,

   $U = n_1 n_2 + \frac{1}{2} n_1 (n_1 + 1) - R_1$

   $= 5 \times 9 + \frac{1}{2} 5 (5 + 1) - 16.5$

   $= 43.5$

   and

   $U = n_1 n_2 + \frac{1}{2} n_2 (n_2 + 1) - R_2$

   $= 5 \times 9 + \frac{1}{2} 9 (9 + 1) - 88.5$

   $= 1.5$

5. Referring to the statistical tables, the lower U value is used, in this case 1.5. In order for it to be significant it must be lower than the critical values in the table. In the significance tables, the value for N_1 and N_2 is 10 at the 0.05 level. Hence, we are more than 95% certain that given the data above, there is a significant difference in the temperature above and below the sewage outlet (since the lower U value – 1.5 – is less than the critical value of 12). We would therefore reject the null hypothesis that states there is no difference in the means of the two samples.

   N.B. There is some variation in the critical values according to different authors.

Activities 5.5

The following data were recorded for carbon emissions (mt per capita) for MEDCs and Emerging economies.

MEDCs	Carbon emissions (mt per capita)	Emerging economies	Carbon emissions (mt per capita)
USA	19.5	China	4.3
Japan	9.6	Russia	10.5
Germany	9.5	India	1.3
Canada	16.1	Mexico	4.1
United Kingdom	9.1	South Africa	8.7
South Korea	9.4	Indonesia	1.9
Italy	7.7	Brazil	1.7
France	6.2	Egypt	2.2
Australia	18.1	Ecuador	2.2

(i)   State the null hypothesis.

(ii) Work out the Mann Whitney statistic.

(iii) State the level of probability of the null hypothesis.

(iv) Accept/reject the null hypothesis.

The Gini Coefficient

The Gini Coefficient is a statistic that measures the degree of similarity between two data sets. It is calculated using the formula: Gini $(G) = \frac{1}{2} \Sigma (X_1 - Y_1)$

Where X and Y are the sets of percentage data. The Gini Coefficient ranges from 0 to 100, with a value of 0 representing identical data and a value of 100 indicating that the data is as different as is possible.

Region	% UK's population	% UK's land	Difference in %s
North West	11.0	3.0	8.0
South East	26.9	11.1	15.8
East	9.2	5.1	4.1
West Midlands	8.8	5.3	3.5
Yorks and Humber	8.3	6.3	2.0
East Midlands	7.1	6.4	0.7
South West	8.3	9.7	1.4
North East	4.0	6.3	2.3
Wales	4.7	8.5	3.8
Northern Ireland	2.8	5.7	2.9
Scotland	8.2	32.2	24.0
			$\Sigma = 68.5$

Gini $(G) = \frac{1}{2} \Sigma (X_1 - Y_1) = \frac{1}{2} \times 68.5 = 34.25$

0 refers to complete similarity and 100 refers to complete concentration (inequality), so this shows that there is some variation in the concentration of people in the UK. It does not have the same impact that a Lorenz curve has, but it is good for comparing different distributions (e.g. income inequality in different countries) or changes over time.

Activities 5.6

The table below shows income inequality in ten countries.

Country	Household income of richest 10%	Household income of poorest 10%
South Africa	51.3	1.2
Zambia	47.4	1.5
Brazil	41.6	1.2
Russia	32.2	2.3
China	31.4	2.1
UK	31.1	1.7
USA	30	2
India	29.8	3.6
Finland	21.5	4.2
Norway	21.2	3.8

Work out the Gini coefficient for income inequality in the above ten countries.

Chapter 6
ICT skills

ICT has come to play an increasingly important role in virtually every subject in the school curriculum. Some skills are of use right across the curriculum while other skills are much more subject specific. The Edexcel Geography specification identifies four particular areas of skill relating to ICT. These are:

- Use of remotely sensed data – photographs, digital images including those captured by satellite.
- Use of databases (digital data), e.g. census data, Environment Agency data; Meteorological Office data.
- Use of geographical information systems (GIS).
- Presentation of text and graphical and cartographic images using ICT.

Photo 6.1: Satellite positioned over the Earth

Use of remotely sensed data

> **Remote sensing:** the science of obtaining information about features on the Earth and other planets from measurements made at a distance.

The essence of remote sensing of the environment is the gathering of information about a place from a distance. It is generally accepted that remote sensing began when Gaspard-Felix Tournachon took aerial photographs of Paris from a hot air balloon in 1858. A few years later in the American Civil War messenger pigeons and unmanned balloons were rigged with cameras to take photographs of enemy positions. The use of air photography for military surveillance expanded rapidly in the First and Second World Wars and in the Cold War that followed. The development of satellites provided a massive advance in the capacity of remote sensing, not only gathering information about the Earth on a global scale, but also providing information about other planets. For example, the Magellan Probe is a satellite that has used remote sensing to create topographic maps of Venus. Remote sensing allows both visible and invisible wavelengths to be monitored.

Photo 6.2: Aerial photograph taken from a hot air balloon of a rural landscape

www.shutterstock.com

Remotely sensed imagery used in conjunction with GIS technology has revolutionised many aspects of geographical analysis. Unprocessed remotely sensed data has many applications, but processing such data digitally can enhance its uses considerably. For example, there are limits to a person's ability to distinguish small differences in colour, but this presents no problem for digital processing. In addition, data sets can be combined, compared and contrasted with great speed and precision.

Remote sensing is largely concerned with reflected radiation. This is the radiation that causes us to see colours, causes infrared film to record vegetation, and allows radar images of the earth to be created. Types of remote sensing data include:

- Radar – used for air traffic control, and the detection of storms and other potential hazards. Radar can also be used to create digital models of elevation.

- Lasers – used in conjunction with satellite radar altimeters to measure wind speed and direction, and the direction of ocean currents. This technology is also used in seafloor mapping.

- Light Detection and Ranging (LIDAR) – used by the military for weapons ranging, but also used to measure chemicals in the atmosphere and the height of ground-based objects.

- Other technologies include stereographic pairs created from multiple air photos to form topographic maps and to view features in 3-D, and air photograph data from earth-viewing satellites.

Cartographers and planners take detailed measurements from aerial photographs in the preparation of maps. Aerial photographs are used to determine land-use and environmental conditions. The interpretation of aerial photographs is a specialised skill which requires considerable training. A significant reason for this is that aerial photographs display a high degree of radial distortion so that corrections need to be made.

In geology, remote sensing can analyse and map large, remote areas. The interpretation of images can help geologists to identify rock types. Remote sensing plays a major role in the analysis of land use. The main use of colour infrared photography is vegetation studies because green vegetation is a very strong reflector of infrared radiation and appears bright red on colour infrared photographs. Urban analysis has come to rely increasingly on remote sensing because it allows planners and other interested parties to identify land uses and land use patterns. This may provide highly relevant data for planning applications.

Landsat

Landsat refers to a series of satellites put into orbit around the earth to collect environmental data with regard to the earth's surface. The program was launched in the early 1970s by the US Department of the Interior and NASA. Later, a similar oceanographic observation satellite program known as SEASAT was launched.

Remote Sensing and GIS

Remotely sensed images have a number of characteristics which make them excellent data sources for geographical information systems. Remote sensing can:

- Provide a wide regional view.
- Provide repetitive coverage of the same area.
- Cover a much broader proportion of the spectrum than the human eye.
- Focus in on a very specific bandwidth in an image.
- Examine a number of bandwidths at the same time.
- Often record signals electronically and provide geo-referenced, digital, data.
- Often operate in all seasons, at night, and in bad weather.

Using remote sensing for A-Level investigations

From the discussion above you can see that there are many possibilities for A-Level students to make use of remote sensing data. You do it already in an indirect way because many of the images that you look at in atlases, textbooks and other geographical materials are the result of remote sensing.

Aerial photographs and satellite images can prove valuable sources of information in field studies because they can show (a) elements of the landscape which are not found on Ordnance Survey maps such as crop distributions and water pollution, and (b) landscape changes by comparing images taken at different times of the year or over longer time periods.

For direct use of remote sensing, satellite images of weather provide a good example linking well with the use of synoptic charts in Chapter 4 of this book. Satellite imagery has revolutionised weather forecasting through the scope and quality of its images and the frequency with which they can be taken. This is how it works:

- A scanner on the satellite called a radiometer sweeps the earth's surface collecting data on how much light is being reflected from surface and atmospheric surfaces.
- The scanner divides the earth's surface into strips and then into pixels similar to a digital image on a computer.
- The data is stored on the satellite and then transmitted to a receiving station on Earth.
- The pixels are reassembled by computer to form an image.

The satellite scanners can pick up visible, infrared and thermal infrared light. Figure 6.1 shows a satellite image of a depression affecting a number of countries in northwest Europe. The clouds are bright white because the cloud tops are at high altitude and are therefore very cold. The infrared image shows this as bright white. You should be able to recognise:

- The front edge of the warm front between Scotland and the southern coast of Norway.
- The back edge of the cold front trailing over the Bay of Biscay and over the northwestern edge of Spain.
- The warm sector which is the mass of white cloud between the warm and cold fronts.
- The hook of the occluded front curling through Ireland.
- The lighter grey clouds following the depression which may indicate rain showers.

Figure 6.1: Infrared satellite image of a depression

In contrast Figure 6.2 shows an area of high pressure over England and Wales in June 2006. It shows:

- Clear conditions across southern and eastern England and across eastern Ireland. Anticyclones are shown by large areas of clear skies. There may be small areas of cloud: these are convectional clouds formed as pockets of hot air rise up through the anticyclone.

- The land surface appears dark because it has been heated by the sun and emits a lot of infrared energy

- The greyer colour of the sea indicated that it is cooler than the land.

- The front approaching from the northwest appears as a bright white band of cloud.

Figure 6.2: Satellite image of an area of high pressure

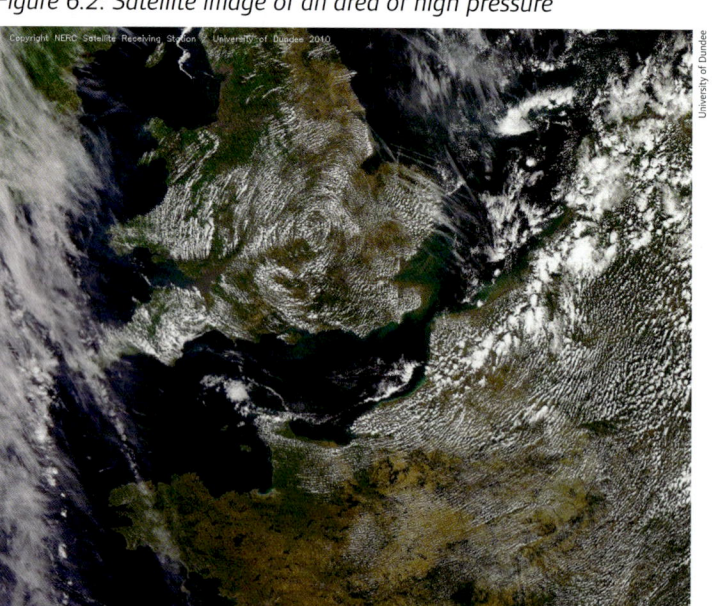

You could track the progression of low and high pressure weather systems in the eastern Atlantic and northwest Europe using both satellite images and synoptic charts, closely correlating the two sources of information. By careful analysis you can show how different climatic conditions affect daily weather events in the UK.

Images from satellite remote sensing websites

Images to enhance geographical investigations can be obtained from a number of websites including:

www.jpl.nasa.gov/radar/sircxsar

https://eros.usgs.gov/satellite-imagery

https://landsat.gsfc.nasa.gov/education/resources/

http://gisgeography.com/free-satellite-imagery-data-list/

Activities 6.1

1. Define remote sensing.

2. What were the first developments in remote sensing?

3. (a) Describe the landscape in Photo 6.2.

   (b) What is the advantage of an aerial photograph like this compared to a photograph taken on the ground?

4. What is the most advanced use of remote sensing today?

5. What is Landsat?

6. Why are remotely sensed images often very good data sources for geographical information systems?

Use of electronic databases

A database: an organised collection of data for one or more purposes, usually in digital form.

Digital databases are an invaluable source of information for geographical analysis. The amount of information of interest to geographers on such databases has increased substantially over the past decade. Access to databases has become an important aspect of geographical enquiry. Here are just a few major sites that have proved useful to students in recent years.

UK National Statistics www.statistics.gov.uk

UK National Statistics provide data on a wide range of themes. There are links to all government departments which are responsible for producing statistics. The themes most likely to be of interest to geographers include:

- **Population:** Population statistics describe the demographic characteristics of the UK population. These include statistics on the size and geographic distribution of the population, on the factors driving population change (births, deaths and migration) and on topics such as families and older people.

- **Migration:** Available information covers migration into and out of the UK, migration within the UK and related matters such as immigration control, asylum, and population by nationality and country of birth.

- **Agriculture and Environment:** information and statistics from across the UK about the agriculture, natural environment, fishing, food and forestry sectors.

- **Energy:** Energy statistics include prices, fuel poverty and energy sources, such as coal or oil.

- **Travel and Transport:** statistics relating to all modes of travel and transport within Great Britain.

Neighbourhood Statistics http://www.neighbourhood.statistics.gov.uk

Neighbourhood Statistics provided by the Office for National Statistics can be an excellent source of information for local enquiries. Some of the most useful features are the downloadable data sets and scale maps which show ward and parish boundaries. Key in a postcode and you can access the database for the

neighbourhood containing that postcode. Figure 6.3 shows the data for Epsom and Ewell 006F, which is part of the Surrey borough of Epsom and Ewell. As you can see from the charts this is an affluent area.

The data from this site can be used for a variety of projects within human geography. You could compare various neighbourhoods within the borough in which you live or analyse a transect from a city centre to the rural-urban fringe to see if the inner city/suburban contrasts you would expect actually exist. You could usefully compare your own fieldwork observations with the picture produced by the neighbourhood statistics. The database allows you to zoom in on maps at a larger and larger scale until you reach the greatest detail the Ordnance Survey can provide. Such maps can act as very useful base maps.

Figure 6.3: Neighbourhood statistics

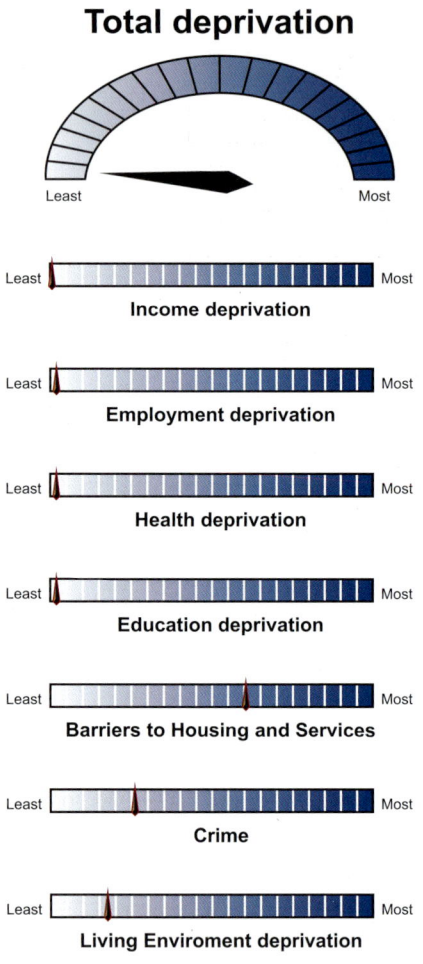

Census data www.ons.gov.uk/census and www.ukcensusonline.com

Censuses continue to be one of the most important tools for understanding human populations scientifically. GIS now plays a key role in census data dissemination and in the analysis of population and household data. Genealogy is one of the fastest growing hobbies in the UK with millions of people using online census databases to research their family histories. Figure 6.4 shows the census information available online from 1841 to 1911. While you may well want to access information from this period for a study in historical geography it is more likely that you will want to access more recent census data. The last census was in March 2011, and is available from https://www.ons.gov.uk/census/2011census. Figure 6.5 shows the hierarchy of census data available which ranges from Government Office Regions to output areas. The latter are geographic areas based on postcodes, averaging about 1,500 people. Smaller-scale investigations often provide more conclusive results than those based at larger scale as well as offering a greater opportunity to include first-hand observation through fieldwork.

Census data can provide the foundation for a range of geographical investigations including:

● Analysing changing population characteristics in selected areas over time.

● Relating population profiles to environmental deprivation/affluence.

● Mapping the spatial distribution of particular ethnic groups.

● Testing hypotheses with regard to processes such as urbanisation, suburbanisation, counter-urbanisation and re-urbanisation.

Figure 6.4: UK Census Online 1841-1911 – the information available

	1841	1851	1861	1871	1881	1891	1901	1911
Name	✓	✓	✓	✓	✓	✓	✓	✓
Age	✓	✓	✓	✓	✓	✓	✓	✓
Sex	✓	✓	✓	✓	✓	✓	✓	✓
Occupation	✓	✓	✓	✓	✓	✓	✓	✓
Address	✓	✓	✓	✓	✓	✓	✓	✓
Place of birth		✓	✓	✓	✓	✓	✓	✓
Relation to head		✓	✓	✓	✓	✓	✓	✓
Marital status		✓	✓	✓	✓	✓	✓	✓
Employment status						✓	✓	✓
Nationality								✓
Duration of current marriage								✓
Number of children born								✓
Number of children living								✓
Number of children dead								✓

Figure 6.5: The hierarchy of census data

Government Office Region (GOR) - nine in England

County (34 counties)

Local authority districts (or unitary authorities/London boroughs)

Upper layer Super Output Area (SOA). Minimum population about 25,000 (Not yet developed)

Middle layer SOA. Minimum population around 5000. Average 7200 (7193 units)

Lower layer SOA. Minimum population around 1000 people, average 1500 (34,378 units)

Output area. Minimum population 100, average 300/125 households (175,434 units)

Increasingly smaller area and higher resolution of data output / detail

Environment Agency data www.environment-agency.gov.uk

The Environment Agency is the public body whose responsibility it is to protect and improve the environment, and to promote sustainable development. The Environment Agency database includes information on:

● flood warning and hydrometric (river and sea level) data;

● environmental facts and figures, including up-to-date information on climate change;

● waste data including information on waste infrastructure and waste management; and

● HiFlow UK providing updated flood peak data at around 1000 river flow gauging stations throughout the UK.

The latter database in particular could provide an invaluable source of information for regional hydrology studies. Grid references are supplied for each gauging station on the database so changes can be observed along a single river and/or comparisons made between a number of rivers.

Meteorological Office data www.metoffice.gov.uk

The Meteorological Office database is a rich source of information on statistics for weather and climate. Figure 6.6 shows the regional data for August 2017. This data is shown in the 'Actual' columns. Variations between the data for 2017 and the average for the period 1981-2010 is shown in the 'Anom' (anomaly) column. So, for example, the average maximum temperature for the UK for August 2017 was 0.5°C cooler

than the long-term average for 1981-2010. Taking all the data together, August 2017 was a relatively cooler and wetter month than the long-term average.

Figure 6.6: Meteorological Office data comparing August 2017 with 1981-2010 average

Region	Max temp		Min temp		Mean temp		Sunshine		Rainfall		Days rain ≥1 mm		Days air frost	
	Actual (°C)	Anom (°C)	Actual (°C)	Anom (°C)	Actual (°C)	Anom (°C)	Actual (°C)	Anom (°C)	Actual (°C)	Anom (°C)	Actual (°C)	Anom (°C)	Actual (°C)	Anom (°C)
UK	18.5	-0.5	10.6	-0.2	14.5	-0.4	159.9	98	104.4	117	14.5	2.5	0.0	0.0
England	20.0	-0.7	11.3	-0.2	15.6	-0.5	181.9	100	74.8	108	11.3	1.3	0.0	0.0
Wales	18.1	-0.8	10.9	-0.1	14.5	-0.5	153.9	92	123.0	115	14.9	2.3	0.0	0.0
Scotland	16.4	-0.2	9.4	0.0	12.9	-0.1	130.5	97	145.1	124	19.1	4.3	0.0	0.0
N Ireland	17.7	-0.4	10.0	-0.5	13.9	-0.5	128.4	95	124.6	128	18.5	3.8	0.0	0.0
England & Wales	19.7	-0.7	11.3	-0.2	15.5	-0.5	178.0	99	81.4	109	11.8	1.5	0.0	0.0
England N	18.8	-0.6	10.8	-0.1	14.8	-0.3	173.6	106	85.9	104	12.2	0.7	0.0	0.0
England S	20.6	-0.8	11.6	-0.3	16.1	-0.5	186.3	97	68.9	111	10.8	1.7	0.0	0.0
Scotland N	15.8	0.0	9.3	0.1	12.5	0.0	116.7	97	157.3	131	21.0	5.1	0.0	0.0
Scotland E	17.0	-0.2	9.0	-0.2	12.9	-0.2	148.7	103	105.6	116	16.2	3.4	0.0	0.0
Scotland W	16.7	-0.4	10.0	0.0	13.3	-0.2	129.7	90	170.5	122	19.5	4.1	0.0	0.0
England E & NE	19.4	-0.4	10.7	-0.1	15.0	-0.3	184.6	109	67.0	97	10.2	-0.2	0.0	0.0
England NW & Wales N	18.0	-0.7	11.1	0.1	14.5	-0.3	149.3	94	120.1	115	15.2	2.1	0.0	0.0
Midlands	19.8	-1.0	11.1	-0.2	15.5	-0.6	178.5	100	70.4	105	11.2	1.2	0.0	0.0
East Anglia	21.6	-0.5	11.9	-0.2	16.7	-0.4	198.8	102	61.7	111	9.1	0.8	0.0	0.0
England SW & Wales S	19.0	-0.8	11.2	-0.4	15.2	-0.6	164.1	89	96.2	107	14.4	3.1	0.0	0.0
England SE & Central S	21.0	-0.8	11.9	-0.2	16.4	-0.5	201.4	99	73.0	127	9.9	1.6	0.0	0.0

Source: Met Office

Digimap www.edina.ac.uk

This is Ordnance Survey map data online. Digimap allows users to view and print maps of any location in Great Britain at a series of predefined scales. Data is available either as maps generated by Digimap online or to download to use with appropriate application software such as GIS or CAD. You must register to use Digimap.

Activities 6.2

1. What is a database?

2. Look at the Neighbourhood Statistics database.

   (a) Enter your postcode to obtain a profile for the area in which you live.

   (b) Obtain a profile for a contrasting residential area by entering an appropriate postcode.

   (c) To what extent do the differences between the two profiles match your perceptions of the differences between the two areas?

Use of geographical information systems

> **Geographical Information System (GIS):** a computer system that allows different types of geographical data to be linked to a location and displayed in an easily understandable form.

"The importance of GIS lies in its ability to combine a wide variety of data to create a spatial picture that is far more useful than the old system of linear comparison."

Reza Firuzabadi, Senior Information Officer, Sustainable Development Network, The World Bank

GIS is a system designed to capture, store, manipulate, analyse, manage, and present all types of geographically referenced data. GIS is used by a wide range of academic disciplines along with an array of public and private organisations. The term 'the geographic approach' is sometimes used to describe the value of this form of analysis (Figure 6.7).

Figure 6.7: The Geographic Approach

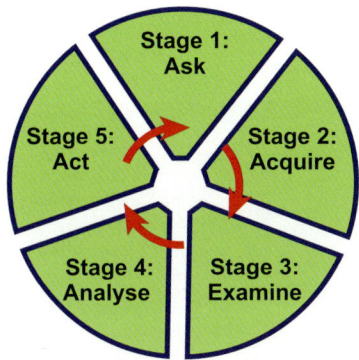

The earliest GIS programmes were very basic compared to their modern counterparts, simply allowing mapped information to be stored in computerised form. GIS made maps easier to store, reproduce and update. The Canadian government developed the first computerised geographical information system in the 1960s which was called the Canada Geographic Information System. It was used to store, analyse and manipulate data for the Canada Land Inventory. This was an attempt to determine the land capability of rural Canada by mapping information relating to soils, agriculture, recreation, wildlife, forestry and land use at a scale of 1: 50,000.

As GIS developed, programmes became more sophisticated with more and more databases being linked to the base maps which are the initial building blocks of such programmes. Each theme or data base such as population density and geology is like a layer of data in map format that is linked geographically to other data layers in a similar format. GIS can project combinations of geographical interrelationships onto a single map or alternatively individual themes can be analysed separately. GIS allows all sorts of information to be visualised on a map so that complex relationships can become apparent in a way that cannot be matched by spreadsheets or tables of statistics. Compared to flat paper maps GIS can produce impressive three-dimensional images and create virtual reality landscapes. Many GIS systems have the capability of incorporating aerial photography, satellite data, and radar imagery into their data layers.

GIS is used advantageously by public and private organisations in virtually every sector of the economy. The benefits of using GIS are:

● Cost savings and increased efficiency.

● Improved decision-making.

● Better communication.

● More efficient record-keeping.

● The much improved ability to manage geographically.

Many aspects of our lives are influenced by GIS without many of us probably realising it:

● Energy companies use GIS for the efficient distribution of power to households and organisations.

● GIS is fundamental to the traffic signal systems that control our roads.

● GIS is responsible for many of the maps that we use on the internet.

● Maps of earthquake shaking hazards are used to create and update building codes in the USA.

● Police forces use GIS to analyse patterns of crime.

● Local authorities can use GIS to identify houses in danger of flooding.

Bing Maps http://www.bing.com/maps/

Bing Maps is a valuable basic GIS resource for fieldwork. It can show how a vertical aerial photograph relates to a map. There are similar tools in Infomapper, Digital Worlds and Aegis 3. The latter in particular is widely used in schools. Bing Maps allows you to print out maps at scales that vary from 1: 40,000,000

to 1: 5,000. For fieldwork purposes you would most likely want to work with maps at a scale of 1: 50,000 or 1: 25,000.

Figure 6.8: Overlaying a scale map onto an aerial photo

Quikmaps http://www.quickmaps.me/

The facility to label features on Google maps makes this a very useful application for creating annotated large-scale local maps or aerial photographs. Various customisable symbols can be added to maps and photographs. Students can export their maps to Google Earth for printing.

Multi-Agency Geographic Information for the Countryside www.magic.gov.uk

This site brings together rural boundaries and information about rural land-based schemes. For the location you select there are many layers of information from the interactive drop-down menu which include:

- Parishes.
- SSSIs.
- Green belt.
- Heritage coast.
- Common land.

A very useful feature of this site is the ability to use maps down to 1: 25,000. The agricultural land classification maps are another feature that could provide the basis for interesting geographical investigations.

Virtual field courses

Virtual field courses provide imaginative ICT opportunities linked to fieldwork providing background information, photographs, virtual tours, clickable maps and other resources relating to local, regional and further-afield places.

Global positioning systems (GPS)

GPS technology can be extremely useful in fieldwork investigations. Data can be recorded along transects or other sampling systems with the position of each point recorded at the same time. GIS-located data can then be fed into a GIS programme, bringing data recording and mapping together.

Figure 6.9 summarises major aspects of GIS in terms of geography fieldwork. A significant attribute of GIS is that it enables the multiple integration of complex data. This is particularly useful when dealing with large data sets.

Figure 6.9: Using GIS in geography fieldwork

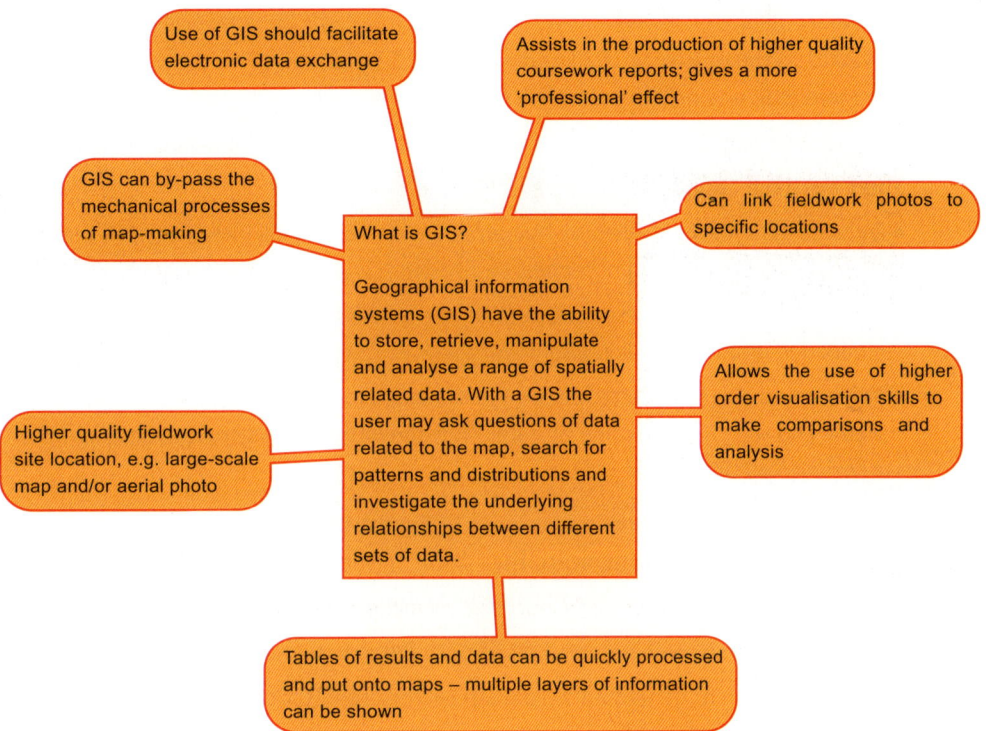

Use of GIS should facilitate electronic data exchange

Assists in the production of higher quality coursework reports; gives a more 'professional' effect

GIS can by-pass the mechanical processes of map-making

Can link fieldwork photos to specific locations

What is GIS?

Geographical information systems (GIS) have the ability to store, retrieve, manipulate and analyse a range of spatially related data. With a GIS the user may ask questions of data related to the map, search for patterns and distributions and investigate the underlying relationships between different sets of data.

Allows the use of higher order visualisation skills to make comparisons and analysis

Higher quality fieldwork site location, e.g. large-scale map and/or aerial photo

Tables of results and data can be quickly processed and put onto maps – multiple layers of information can be shown

---

Activities 6.3

1. What is a geographical information system?

2. When was GIS first developed?

3. Give three advantages of GIS to public and private organisations.

4. State three ways of using GIS which are of interest to geographers.

Use of innovative sources of data

With the rapid advance of technology new sources of data and the ability to analyse such data have emerged. The most widely known of these new data sources are 'big data' and 'crowdsourcing'. The fact that these terms did not appear in the previous Edexcel Geography syllabus are a good indication of how relatively recent they are. While big data and crowdsourcing are separate phenomena, there is a clear area of overlap as one of the ways big data can be obtained is from crowdsourcing! The data that has been collected from these sources covers a wide range of subjects and topics. Some are clearly geographical in nature, others are not.

> **Big data:** extremely large data sets analysed computationally to reveal patterns, trends and associations.

The term 'big data' emerged in the mid-1990s when it was first used to describe the handling and analysis of huge databases. However, the term did not become widely used until more than ten years later. These data sets were often too large and complex for traditional data processing software. Such large data sets that are analysed computationally can reveal patterns and trends which otherwise might remain understood to a lesser degree. The analysis of big data has been particularly successful with regard to enhancing the understanding of human behaviour and interactions. Big data has become increasingly thought of as a 'social phenomenon' in its own right. Advocates of big data see it as playing a major role in how organisations solve global problems in the future. It can be seen as being fundamental in the movement from data-scarce to data-rich studies of a wide range of national and global issues.

Examples of big data include:

- In 2012, Walmart was generating more than 2.5 petabytes (2 to the power of 50 bytes) of data relating to more than one million customer transactions every hour

- In the same year, Facebook was processing 2.5 billion pieces of content every day.

There are three basic methods of collecting big data:

- Directed systems: controlled by human operators. Examples include closed-circuit television and LiDAR (light detection and ranging) scans.

- Automated systems: These include Internet banking, sending emails and measurements from sensors embedded into objects or environments.

- Volunteered systems: these rely on system users to provide data. Examples include engaging in social media and the crowdsourcing of data. With the latter, users generate data and then contribute them to a common platform.

Because of the huge volumes and velocity of big data, the big questions are (a) how to make sense of the data and (b) how to communicate that sense. Visualisation and mapping have proved to be essential techniques in this quest. An example is the continual monitoring of the flow of traffic in an urban area.

There are of course some potential disadvantages of big data:

- Most big data are generated by private sector organisations and they therefore decide the extent to which such data is shared.

- There may be concerns about how clean (errors and gaps), objective (bias-free) and consistent (few discrepancies) data sets are.

- There are ethical questions such as the infringement of individual privacy, along with security concerns.

- Big data should not be viewed as a substitute for traditional data collection and analysis, but rather as a supplement to it.

> **Crowdsourcing:** engaging a 'crowd' to contribute data on a volunteer basis for a common good.

The term 'crowdsourcing' was first used in 2005. It is a portmanteau of 'crowd' and 'sourcing'. Crowdsourcing is obtaining information on a volunteer basis from a large group (crowd) of people online. The principle behind it is that by asking a large crowd of people for information, ideas, skills etc, the quality of the response will be superior to more traditional sources of data. Crowdsourcing is distinct from outsourcing as the information comes from an undefined public as opposed to being commissioned from a specific named group. The setting up of a crowdsourcing task and the analysis of the data it brings in is usually organised by relevant professionals while the sources of information are mainly from volunteer enthusiasts. Thus, the phenomenon is a mixture of bottom-up and top-down processes. Advocates of crowdsourcing stress its:

- Low cost
- Flexibility
- Speed
- Scalability
- Quality

The most famous example of crowdsourcing is Wikipedia, the free online encyclopedia. Created in 2001 it is written collaboratively by volunteers who write without pay. Wikipedia has about 70,000 active contributors.

An interesting study into the efficiency of crowdsourcing was carried out recently by the University of Colorado Boulder. The task was mapping craters on the moon. The work of 8 NASA scientists was compared with a group of thousands of amateur enthusiasts who counted craters via the crowd-source gathering place 'CosmoQuest'. Each group counted the number of craters larger than 35ft in diameter. The results of both groups were analysed and they were found to be statistically the same!

In Boston, the city council designed a fully-integrated smartphone app for citizens to report issues such as graffiti and potholes. A significant number of people provided relevant information enabling the council to tackle problems before they got worse, reducing maintenance costs and potential litigation.

Crowdsourcing has proved to be important in the emergency response to many different types of natural disaster including flooding and wildfires where observations from a large number of individuals spread over a significant geographic area can provide vital information at high speed for those directing emergency response.

Two important concepts linked to crowdsourcing are crowdfunding and microtasking. Crowdfunding involves asking a crowd of people to donate money to a particular project. Such projects are frequently humanitarian or environmental. Microtasking involves dividing a body of work up into tiny tasks and sending these small tasks out to different groups (crowds) of people.

Presentation of text and graphical and cartographic images using ICT

Developing and using ICT skills appropriately will allow students to complete geographical enquiries more efficiently and effectively, resulting in better time management. When you are ready to present your work you will have choices to make with regard to how you choose to use and organise the text and illustrations. Making the right choices is important if you are to produce a good piece of geographical analysis which shows clear sequence and progression in description, explanation/analysis, conclusion and evaluation.

Most students will be very familiar with the different possibilities of presenting text using ICT by the time they reach A-level, having acquired a range of skills at earlier stages in their education. The most basic reasons for using word processing are:

- An investigation that is word processed will generally look better than one which is handwritten

- It is much easier to edit mistakes on a computer than in a handwritten investigation.

- Spreadsheets allow the clear presentation of tables and make calculations easy.

- Presentation using a computer allows students to collect, display, communicate and evaluate findings in a creative and personal fashion.

- It aids the integration of text and illustrations. The ability to easily move illustrations as the text develops is an important and valuable aspect of editing.

Spreadsheets can be an extremely useful tool for data processing, particularly when handling large data sets. Spreadsheets can also be used to aid data entry, for example following a group data-collecting exercise. The 'sharing' facility in Excel allows a number of people/computers to use the same spreadsheet. This is very effective for rapid data entry over a number of networked machines. Reference has already been made to the valuable role of spreadsheets in data presentation.

ICT provides access to a wide range of free web-based digital maps of differing types and scales alongside aerial and satellite images. Different images can be compared quickly to assess their suitability for the task in hand. This is extremely helpful in assessing the relationship or correlation between different types of image, for example, linking a satellite image to an Ordnance Survey map. ICT provides access to historical geography, via archive materials, for example the materials available on the RGS-IBG website.

Graphical and cartographic images: selecting appropriate techniques

Modern computers provide students with a wide variety of graphical techniques, but the decision-making lies with the user. Selecting an inappropriate graphical technique can confuse your description and explanation rather than enhancing it. Think carefully about each illustration you intend to use and ask yourself if it is appropriate for the purpose of the investigation. If it is appropriate, is it the best type of illustration to use for the task in hand. It may be that two or three types of technique are valid, but that it is not too difficult to prioritise them with one particular technique being better than the alternatives for what you want to do!

A common mistake is to try to use as many different techniques as possible, but this may lead to similar data being presented in different ways for the sake of it rather than actually enhancing the overall analysis. You should be able to clearly justify the use of all the graphical and cartographic techniques that you include in your enquiry. All your illustrations should be clear and easy to understand. They should be fully integrated with the text.

Google Earth https://www.google.co.uk/intl/en_uk/earth/

Google Earth allows the user to fly anywhere to view satellite imagery, maps, terrain, 3D buildings, galaxies in outer space and the depths of the ocean. You can also travel back in time with Historical Imagery in Google Earth to see how your local area and other places have changed over time.

Google Earth offers the means to display geographic data from a wide variety of sources together in a geospatial context. This data includes imagery for the entire globe at varying resolutions that contains a great deal of interpretable visual information. Students can use it to find their homes, schools, and other locations that are familiar to them. They can make inferences by comparing familiar places to other locations. In addition, students can learn about the world through rich layers of mappable data offered. They can also create and display their own data.

And finally

Ensure that you keep a back-up copy of your work! It is easy to think that work will never be lost on a computer, but it happens more frequently than you might think.

Chapter 7
Statistical tables

Statistical tables

Student's t-distribution

Values of t corresponding to 95% and 99% probability and degrees of freedom.

Degrees of Freedom	95%	99%
1	12.71	63.66
2	4.30	9.93
3	3.18	5.84
4	2.78	4.60
5	2.57	4.03
6	2.45	3.71
7	2.37	3.50
8	2.31	3.36
9	2.26	3.25
10	2.23	3.17
11	2.20	3.11
12	2.18	3.06
13	2.16	3.01
14	2.15	2.98
15	2.13	2.95
16	2.12	2.92
17	2.11	2.90
18	2.10	2.88
19	2.09	2.86
20	2.09	2.85
21	2.08	2.83
22	2.07	2.82
23	2.07	2.81
24	2.06	2.80
25	2.06	2.79
26	2.06	2.78
27	2.05	2.77
28	2.05	2.76
29	2.04	2.76
30	2.04	2.75
40	2.02	2.70
60	2.00	2.66

Spearman's Rank Correlation Coefficient

The critical values for Spearman's rank for N = 4 to N = 30, at the 95% (0.05) and 99% (0.01) levels of significance. The greater the value of Rs the more significant the result. For numbers of pairs greater than 30 the critical value of Rs decreases only slightly.

N	Significance level 95%	99%
4	1.00	
5	0.90	1.00
6	0.83	0.94
7	0.71	0.89
8	0.64	0.83
9	0.60	0.78
10	0.56	0.75
12	0.50	0.71
14	0.46	0.65

N	Significance level 95%	99%
16	0.43	0.60
18	0.40	0.56
20	0.38	0.53
22	0.36	0.51
24	0.34	0.49
26	0.33	0.47
28	0.32	0.45
30	0.31	0.43

Chi squared test (X^2)

The critical values show the probability that the calculated value of X^2 is the result of a chance distribution. The larger the value of X^2 the smaller is the probability that the null hypothesis is correct.

df	95%	99%
1	3.84	6.64
2	5.99	9.21
3	7.82	11.34
4	9.49	13.28
5	11.07	15.09
6	12.59	16.81
7	14.07	18.48
8	15.51	20.09
9	16.92	21.67
10	18.31	23.21
11	19.68	24.72
12	21.03	26.22
13	22.36	27.69
14	23.68	29.14
15	25.00	30.58
16	26.30	32.00
17	27.59	33.41
18	28.87	34.80
19	30.14	36.19
20	31.41	37.57

Critical tables for Mann Whitney

The calculated value of U must be less than the critical values if U is to be regarded as significant.

95% level of significance

	N₁ = 2	3	4	5	6	7	8	9	10	11	12	13	14	15	16	17	18	19	20
N₂ = 3	0	1	1	2	3	3	4	5	5	6	6	7	8	8	9	10	10	11	12
4	0	1	2	3	4	5	6	7	8	9	10	11	12	13	15	16	17	18	19
5	1	2	3	5	6	7	9	10	12	13	14	16	17	19	20	21	23	24	26
6	1	3	4	6	8	9	11	13	15	17	18	20	22	24	26	27	29	31	33
7	1	3	5	7	9	12	14	16	18	20	22	25	27	29	31	34	36	38	40
8	2	4	6	9	11	14	16	19	21	24	27	29	32	34	37	40	42	45	48
9	2	5	7	10	13	16	19	22	25	28	31	34	37	40	43	46	49	52	55
10	2	5	8	12	15	18	21	25	28	32	35	38	42	45	49	52	56	59	63
11	2	6	9	13	17	20	24	28	32	35	39	43	47	51	55	58	62	66	70
12	3	6	10	14	18	22	27	31	35	39	43	48	52	56	61	65	69	73	78
13	3	7	11	16	20	25	29	34	38	43	48	52	57	62	66	71	76	81	85
14	4	8	12	17	22	27	32	37	42	47	52	57	62	67	72	78	83	88	93
15	4	8	13	19	24	29	34	40	45	51	56	62	67	73	78	84	89	95	101
16	4	9	15	20	26	31	37	43	49	55	61	66	72	78	84	90	96	102	108
17	4	10	16	21	27	34	40	46	52	58	65	71	78	84	90	97	103	110	116
18	5	10	17	23	29	36	42	49	56	62	69	76	83	89	96	103	110	117	124
19	5	11	18	24	31	38	45	52	59	66	73	81	88	95	102	110	117	124	131
20	5	12	19	26	33	40	48	55	63	70	78	85	93	101	108	116	124	131	139

99% level of significance

	N₁ = 2	3	4	5	6	7	8	9	10	11	12	13	14	15	16	17	18	19	20
N₂ = 3	0	0	0	0	0	1	1	2	2	2	3	3	3	4	4	5	5	5	6
4	0	0	0	1	2	2	3	4	4	5	6	6	7	8	9	9	10	10	11
5	0	0	1	2	3	4	5	6	7	8	9	10	11	12	13	14	15	16	17
6	0	0	2	3	4	5	7	8	9	10	12	13	14	16	17	19	20	21	23
7	0	1	2	4	5	7	8	10	12	13	15	17	18	20	22	24	25	27	29
8	0	1	3	5	7	8	10	12	14	16	18	21	23	25	27	29	31	33	35
9	0	2	4	6	8	10	12	15	17	19	22	24	27	29	32	34	37	39	41
10	0	2	4	7	9	12	14	17	20	23	25	28	31	34	37	39	42	45	48
11	0	2	5	8	10	13	16	19	23	26	29	32	35	38	42	45	48	51	54
12	0	3	6	9	12	15	18	22	25	29	32	36	39	43	47	50	54	57	61
13	1	3	6	10	13	17	21	24	28	32	36	40	44	48	52	56	60	64	68
14	1	3	7	11	14	18	23	27	31	35	39	44	48	52	57	61	66	70	74
15	1	4	8	12	16	20	25	29	34	38	43	48	52	57	62	67	71	76	81
16	1	4	8	13	17	22	27	32	37	42	47	52	57	62	67	72	77	83	87
17	1	5	9	14	19	24	29	34	39	45	50	56	61	67	72	78	83	89	94
18	1	5	10	15	20	25	31	37	42	48	54	60	66	71	77	83	89	95	101
19	2	5	10	16	21	27	33	39	45	51	57	64	70	76	83	89	95	102	108
20	2	6	11	17	23	29	35	41	48	54	61	68	74	81	88	94	101	108	115

Chapter 8
Answers

Chapter 2

Activities 2.1

1. (a) Student exercise: look at the school site from various angles. Views from upstairs classrooms might be particularly helpful. Note the relative sizes of the buildings and outdoor areas and try to show these differences with reasonable accuracy on your base map.

   (b) Provide accurate labels, for example, 'science block', 'administration block'.

   (c) An example might be 'Humanities building where Geography, History and Religious Studies are taught'.

2. Descriptive annotation – 'upper course of a river valley with V-shape and steep sides'.

   Descriptive and explanatory annotation – 'upper course of a river valley with a V-shape and steep sides as a result of pronounced vertical erosion'.

Activities 2.2

1. A hand-drawn summary of an environment you are looking at.

2. Look for a clear sketch map showing a good range of features with clear use of labels, descriptive annotations and some degree of explanatory annotation.

Activities 2.3

1. Different sets of information drawn on separate clear plastic sheets that can be placed on top of each other to form a coherent map or diagram.

2. Allow one layer of information to be drawn on a clear surface without the information contained in the other layers getting in the way. A good method to illustrate patterns and relationships in human and physical landscapes. A visually impressive technique when well constructed.

Activities 2.4

1. (a) Coding involves searching a text for similar themes, concepts and key words and marking the relevant areas of the text with a code colour.

   (b) A text could be divided into three colours showing the (i) causes (ii) consequences and (iii) potential solutions to an environmental problem.

2. The four types of measurement are nominal, ordinal (ranked), interval and ratio.

Activities 2.5

1. A good questionnaire has a limited number of questions that take a short time to answer; is carefully worded so that the respondents are clear about the meaning of each question; and, follows a logical sequence so that respondents can see 'where the questionnaire is going'.

2. Closed questions only allow the respondent to answer one of the pre-set answers whereas an open question allows the respondent to reply in no predetermined way.

3. An interview is more detailed than a questionnaire. It also involves a smaller number of respondents, is more of a discussion than a questionnaire and is likely to have more open-ended questions than a questionnaire.

Activities 2.6

1. (a) Northings are the horizontal grid lines. They increase in value from south to north.

   (b) Eastings are the vertical grid lines on maps. They increase in value from west to east.

2. A – 6313; B – 6712; C – 6614; D – 6416.

3. A – 638128; B – 675125; C – 659144; D – 675168.

Activities 2.7

1. Low-lying land at and around 20m forms a much larger part of this landscape than higher land at and around 60m altitude.

2. The standard distance between each contour.

3. These are major contours which are depicted at 50m intervals on 1: 50,000 OS maps.

4. Spot heights, triangulation pillars, bench marks.

5. (a) 257848; (b) Tourist information centre, a country park, camping and caravanning sites, a museum and a Roman fort; (c) a Roman fort; (d) 3 km.

Activities 2.8

1. A finger of higher land projecting out into a valley.

2. A river.

3. A clinometer.

4. Refer to the labels below each of the four diagrams in Figure 2.14.

5. (a) An escarpment has two contrasting slopes. On one side is the steep scarp slope and on the other side the more gentle dip slope.

   (b) Starting in the west, add the 90m, 110m, 120m and 130m labels to the west of the highest land. From the 140m contour to the east add labels for the 130m, 120m, 110m and 90m contours.

6. (a) The degree to which a slope inclines.

   (b) Divide the difference in horizontal distance (D) by the height (H). If the answer is, for example, '10' express it as '1:10'.

Chapter 3

Activities 3.1

1. (a) southwest; (b) south-southeast; (c) east-northeast; (d) northwest; (e) southwest.

2. (a) north-northeast; (b) east-southeast; (c) northeast; (d) south-southwest.

3. (a) Direction relative to North as indicated by a compass.

   (b) A bearing is measured in degrees in a clockwise direction from North which is 0°.

4. NNE – 22.5°; ENE – 67.5°; ESE – 112.5°; SSE – 157.5°; SSW – 202.5°; WSW – 247.5°; WNW – 292.5°; NNW – 337.5°.

Activities 3.2

1. (a) 0°; (b) 23.5°N; (c) 23.5°S; (d) 66.5°N; (E) 66.5°S.

2. (a) The Equator is exactly between the North Pole and the South Pole.

   (b) the most northerly position where the sun shines directly down onto the earth's surface at an angle of 90°.

(c) the most southerly position where the sun shines directly down on the earth's surface at an angle of 90°.

(d) the most southerly point in the northern hemisphere which experiences a complete 24 hour period of daylight during the summer solstice in the Northern Hemisphere.

(e) the most northerly point in the southern hemisphere which experiences a complete 24 hour period of daylight during the summer solstice in the Southern Hemisphere.

3. (a) 35.40°N 139.45°E; (b) 43.00°N 75.00°W; (c) 55.45°N 37.42°E; (d) 39.55°N 116.25°E.

Activities 3.3

1. 53.18°N 4.38°W.

2. 130 miles/210 km.

3. Generally above 200m with a number of smaller isolated areas above 500m. Over half a dozen peaks are in excess of 700m. Only two peaks, Snowdon and Carnedd Llewelyn exceed 1000m.

Activities 3.4

1. A distance of 1000 km or more which corresponds to the scale typical of depressions and anticyclones in mid-latitudes.

2. Midnight, 6.00 a.m., midday, and 6.00 p.m.

3. (a) It is centred over southern Scandinavia and the northern part of the North Sea.

(b) As far as north Africa.

(c) Temperate is 12°C; 3/8 cloud cover (three oktas); fog; calm conditions; high pressure between 1024 and 1032 mb.

4. (a) To the WNW of Ireland.

(b) Eastwards.

(c) Anticlockwise.

(d) Temperature is 11°C; full cloud cover (8/8); south-westerly wind at 18-22 knots; low pressure at approximately 986 mb.

Activities 3.5

1. The proportional circles should have radii of 2cm, 3cm, and 4cm following the third column in Figure 3.12.

2. (a) Uniformly thin and straight lines to link points of origin and destination.

(b) For example, to show where shoppers in a market town live.

3. Flows lines follow actual routes while desire lines are drawn directly from the point of origin to the point of destination.

Activities 3.6

1. (a) France and Iceland are the only countries in the highest class with a total fertility rate of over 2.0. Norway, Sweden and the Republic of Ireland are all in the second highest class between 1.75 and 2.00. The UK, the Netherlands, Denmark and Finland are all in the middle class with total fertility rates between 1.50 and 1.74. All the other European countries shown on the map fall into the two lowest classes. These countries are all in central, southern and eastern Europe.

(b) They can show abrupt changes at boundary lines when in reality change is much more gradual.

2. The map shows concentrations of sulphur dioxide ranging from below 100μg/m^3 to over 800μg/m^3. The pattern is elongated from north-east to south-west, possibly due to wind patterns.

Chapter 4

Activities 4.1
Global population

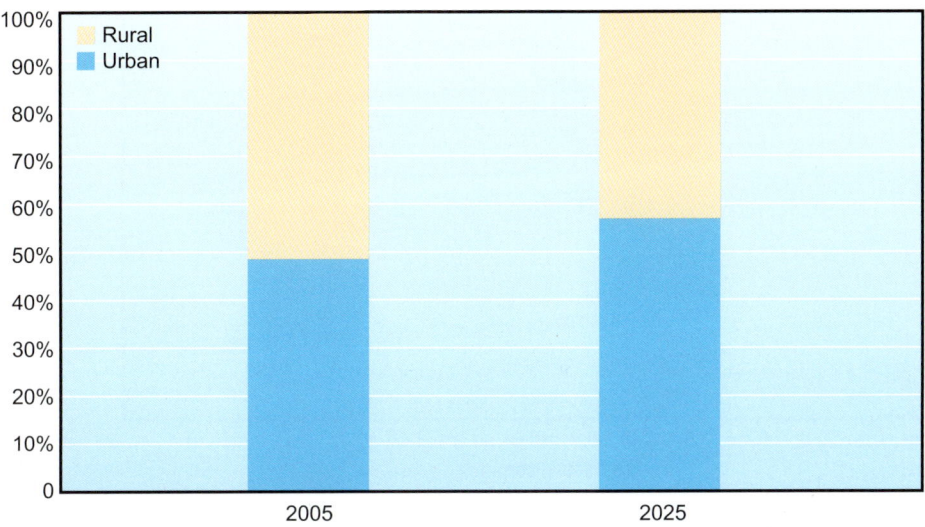

Activities 4.2
Pie chart of London's ecological footprint

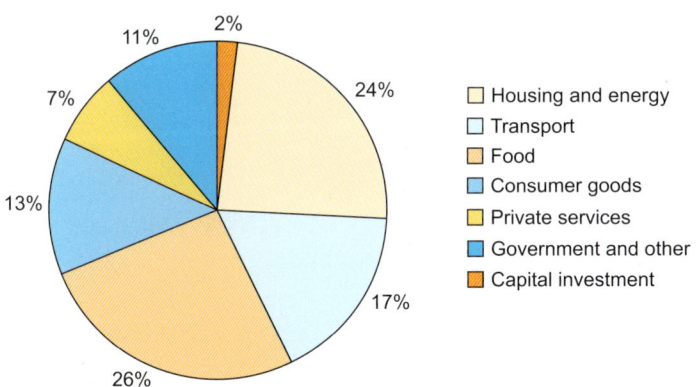

Activities 4.3

Proportional pie charts to show the number of inhabitants in cities of different sizes, 2005 and 2025

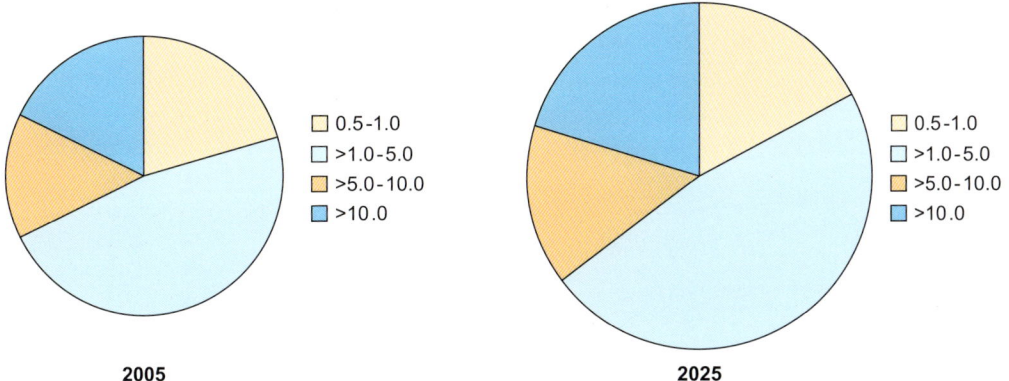

Activities 4.4
Scatter graph to show relationship between discharge and suspended load

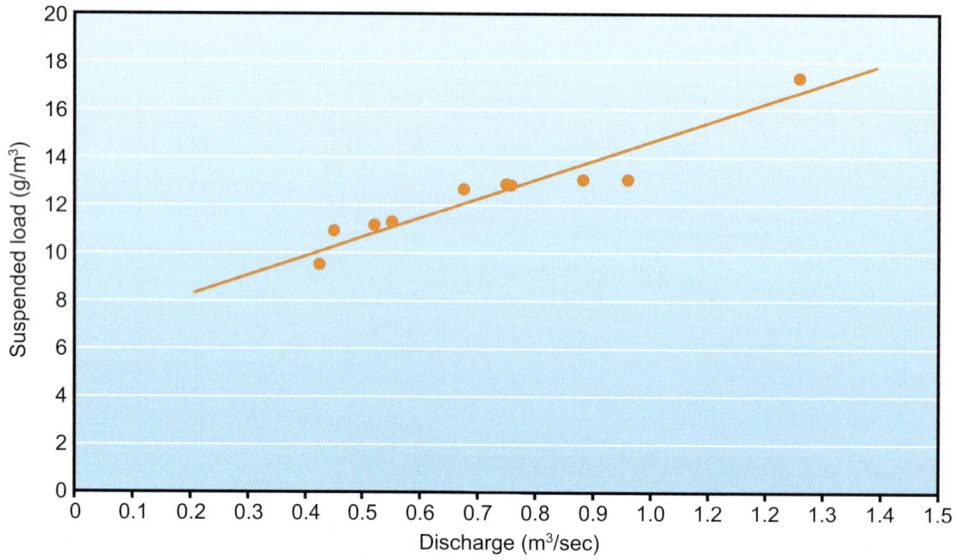

Activities 4.5
Triangular graph to show changes in Korea's employment structure

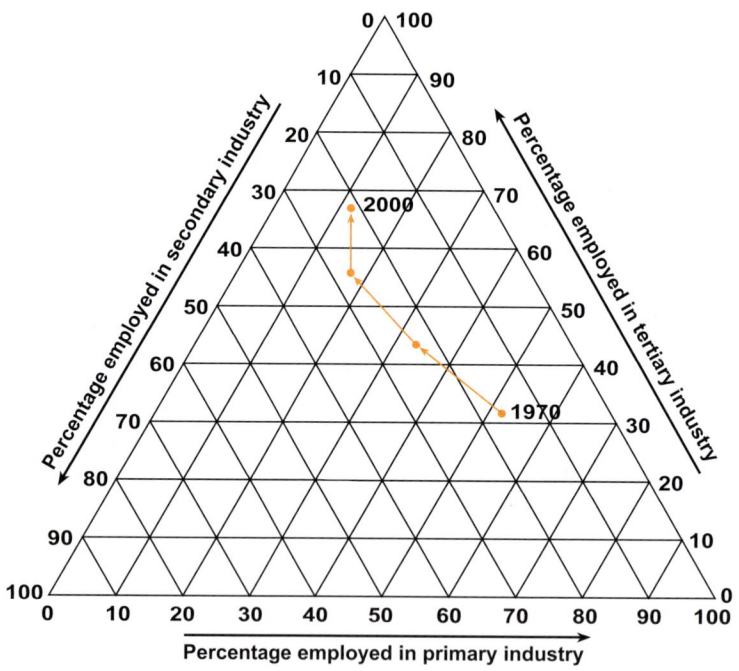

Activities 4.6

Lorenz curve to show wealth inequality in selected countries

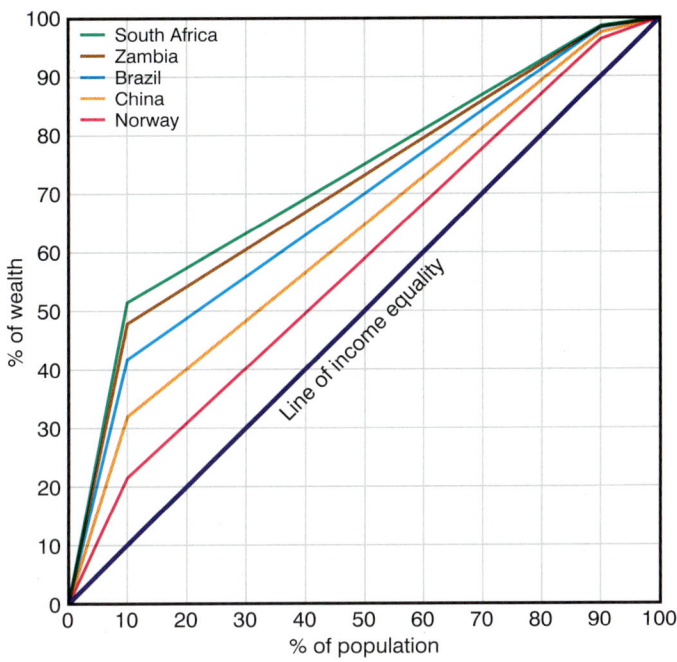

Chapter 5

Activities 5.1 – Standard deviation

(i) The **maximum** is 752 mm, the **minimum** is 471 mm and the **range** is thus from 752 to 471 mm, i.e. 281.

(ii) The **interquartile range** is 672.5 - 577.5 = 95.

(iii) The mean is 615.2 mm and the standard deviation is 77.36 mm.

(iv) This gives a much more accurate figure than the range or the interquartile range, as it takes into account all values and is not as affected by extreme values.

(v) Given normal probability we would expect that c.68% of the observations will fall within 1 standard deviation of the mean, c.95% within 2 standard deviations of the mean, and c. 99% within 3 standard deviations.

Activities 5.2 – Spearman's rank

(i) The null hypothesis states that there is no relationship between gross national income and life expectancy.

Country	Gross national income ($)	Life expectancy	Rank GNI	Rank Life expectancy	Difference in ranks	Difference^2
Luxemburg	70,529	79.03	1	3	-2	4
Norway	46,154	79.67	2	2	0	0
Finland	33,674	78.66	3	4	-1	1
Bahrain	25,431	79.78	4	1	3	9
Estonia	20,404	72.30	5	13	-8	64
Saudi Arabia	13,267	75.88	6	7	-1	1
Malaysia	12,642	76.96	7	5	2	4
Uruguay	10,847	75.95	8	6	2	4
Mexico	10,570	75.63	9	8	1	1
Turkey	8,932	72.88	10	=11.5	-1.5	2.25
Dom. Rep.	8,231	73.07	11	10	1	1
China	7,693	72.88	12	=11.5	0.5	0.25
El Salvador	4,847	71.78	13	14	-1	1
Jamaica	4,611	73.12	14	9	5	25
Morocco	4,517	71.22	15	15	0	0
India	3,678	68.59	16	16	0	0
Ghana	2,616	59.12	17	18	-1	1
Zimbabwe	2,059	38.50	18	20	-2	4
Ethiopia	978	49.23	19	19	0	0
Madagascar	887	62.14	20	17	3	9
						$\Sigma D^2 = 131.5$

(ii) $1 - (6 \Sigma D^2)/(n^3 - n) =$

$1 - (6 \times 131.5)/(20^3 - 20) = 1 - (789/7980) =$

$1 - 0.098 = 1 - 0.1 = 0.9$

(iii) It is a positive relationship i.e. as gross national income increases so does life expectancy.

(iv) It is 99% significant – the null hypothesis can therefore be rejected.

Activities 5.3 – X^2

1. (i) There is no difference in the number of cirques found at different altitudes.

(ii)

Altitude (m)	No. of cirques (Obs.)	Expected no. of cirques (Exp)	(O-E)	(O-E)^2	(O-E)^2/E
> 1100	36	7	29	841	120.1
900-1100	18	14	4	16	1.1
700-899	11	21	10	100	4.8
500-699	5	28	23	529	18.9
Total	**70**				**Σ144.9**

(iii) 144.9.

(iv) 99%, i.e. there is a significant difference in the number of cirques and altitudes i.e. there are much more at higher altitudes.

(v) Reject the null hypothesis.

2. (i) There is no difference in the type of soils found on the different bedrocks.

(ii) Expected frequencies

	Podzol	**Brown earth**	**Gley**
Sandstone	44 x 58/100 = 25.22	30 x 58/100 = 17.4	26 x 58/100 = 15.08
Shale	44 x 42/100 = 18.48	30 x 42/100 = 12.6	26 x 42/100 = 10.92

(iii) Working out the X^2 statistic

	Obs (O)	**Exp (E)**	**(O-E)**	**(O-E)^2**	**(O-E)^2/E**
Sandstone/podzol	31	25.5	5.5	30.25	1.2
Sandstone/brown earth	19	17.4	-1.6	2.56	0.1
Sandstone/gley	8	15.1	-7.1	50.41	3.3
Shale/podzol	13	18.5	-5.5	30.25	1.6
Shale/brown earth	11	12.6	1.6	2.56	0.2
Shale/gley	18	10.9	7.1	50.41	4.6

Σ (o-e)^2/e = 11.0

Degrees of freedom = (r-1) x (k-1) = (3-1) x (2-1)-(2) x (1) = 2 degrees of freedom.

(iv) The result is significant at the 99% level of significance i.e. there is a significant difference in the type of soil and bedrock.

(v) Reject the null hypothesis.

Activities 5.4 – Nearest neighbour statistic

Marsh

Vegetation type	**Neighest neighbour**	**Distance (m)**
1	2	10
2	1, 3	10
3	2, 4, 5	10
4	3, 6	10
5	3, 6	10
6	4, 5	10
		Σd = 60

Formula

NNI or Rn = 2 $\sqrt{(N/A)}$

= Σd/N = 60/6 = 10

Rn = 2 x 10 x $\sqrt{(6/13,200)}$

Rn = 0.43

Woodland

Vegetation type	Neighest neighbour	Distance (m)
1	2	14
2	3	10
3	2	10
4	6	20
5	6	10
6	5, 7	10
7	6	10
8	9	10
9	8	10
10	9	20
11	7	22
12	14	30
13	14	30
14	13	30
		$\Sigma d = 236$

Formula

NNI or Rn = $2 \sqrt{(N/A)}$

= $\Sigma d/N$ = 236/14 = 16.86

Rn = 2 x 16.86 x $\sqrt{(14/13,200)}$

Rn = 1.10

Activities 5.5 – Mann Whitney test

(i) The null hypothesis, H_0, states that there is no significant difference in the structure of the two samples, *i.e.* there is no significant difference in the carbon emissions of MEDCs and emerging economies.

(ii)

MEDCs	Rank of carbon emissions (mt per capita)	Emerging economies	Rank of carbon emissions (mt per capita)
USA	18	China	7
Japan	14	Russia	15
Germany	13	India	1
Canada	16	Mexico	6
United Kingdom	11	South Africa	10
South Korea	12	Indonesia	3
Italy	9	Brazil	2
France	8	Egypt	4.5
Australia	17	Ecuador	4.5
	$\Sigma = 118$		$\Sigma = 53$

$U_1 = n_1n_2 + \frac{1}{2}n\ (n_1+1) - R_1$

Or

$U_2 = n_1n_2 + \frac{1}{2}n_2\ (n_2 + 1) - R_2$

Thus $U_1 = 9 \times 9 + \frac{1}{2} \times 9\ (10) - 118 = 81 + 45 - 118 = 126 - 118 = 8$

And $U_2 = 9 \times 9 + \frac{1}{2} \times 9\ (10) - 53 = 81 + 45 - 53 = 126 - 53 = 73$

(iii) At the 95% level of significance = 22, therefore we can be 95% confident that there is a significant difference between the carbon emissions of rich countries (MEDCs) compared with emerging economies. It is also significant at the 99% level of significance.

(iv) The null hypothesis is rejected *i.e.* there is a significant difference in the emissions of MEDCs and emerging economies.

Activities 5.6 – Gini coefficient

South Africa: $G = \frac{1}{2}\ ((51-10) + (80-47.8) + (10-1.2)) = \frac{1}{2}\ (41 + 32.2 + 8.3) = 41$

Zambia	$= \frac{1}{2}\ ((47.4-10) + (80-51.1) + (10-1.5)) = \frac{1}{2}\ (37.4 + 28.9 + 8.5) = 37.4$
Brazil	$= \frac{1}{2}\ ((41.6-10) + (80-53.2) + (10-1.2)) = \frac{1}{2}\ (31.6 + 26.8 + 8.8) = 33.6$
Russia	$= \frac{1}{2}\ ((32.2-10) + (80-65.5) + (10-2.3)) = \frac{1}{2}\ (22.2 + 14.5 + 7.3) = 22$
China	$= \frac{1}{2}\ ((31.4-10) + (80-66.5) + (10-2.1)) = \frac{1}{2}\ (21.4 + 13.5 + 7.9) = 21.4$
UK	$= \frac{1}{2}\ ((31.1-10) + (80-67.2) + (10-1.7)) = \frac{1}{2}\ (21.1 + 12.8 + 8.3) = 21.1$
USA	$= \frac{1}{2}\ ((30-10) + (80-68) + (10-2)) = \frac{1}{2}\ (20 + 12 + 8) = 20$
India	$= \frac{1}{2}\ ((29.8-10) + (80-66.6) + (10-3.6)) = \frac{1}{2}\ (19.8 + 13.4 + 6.4) = 19.8$
Finland	$= \frac{1}{2}\ ((21.5-10) + (80-74.3) + (10-4.2)) = \frac{1}{2}\ (11.5 + 5.7 + 5.8) = 11.5$
Norway	$= \frac{1}{2}\ ((21.2-10) + (80-75) + 10-3.8)) = \frac{1}{2}\ (11.2 + 5 + 6.2) = 11.2$

Chapter 6

Activities 6.1

1. The gathering of information about a place from a distance.

2. In 1858 when Gaspard-Felix Tournachon took aerial photographs of Paris from a hot air balloon and a few years later in the American Civil War when messenger pigeons and unmanned balloons were rigged with cameras to take photographs of enemy positions.

3. (a) The landscape is a fairly even mix of urban and rural land uses with the former being mainly in the foreground. Arable farming is clearly in evidence along with a considerable wooded area.

   (b) Aerial photos can generally cover a wider area and therefore show much greater contrast than photographs taken from the ground unless the latter is from an exceptional vantage point.

4. Gathering information about other planets.

5. A series of satellites put into orbit around the earth to collect environmental data with regard to the earth's surface – launched in the early 1970s by the US Department of the Interior and NASA.

6. Provides a wide regional view and repetitive coverage of the same area. Covers a much broader proportion of the spectrum than the human eye. Can focus in on a very specific bandwidth in an image or examine a number of bandwidths at the same time. Often records signals electronically and provide geo-referenced, digital, data. The ability to often operate in all seasons, at night, and in bad weather.

Activities 6.2

1. An organised collection of data for one or more purposes, usually in digital form.

2. Student exercise depending on choice of neighbourhoods. The exercise should ensure that all 8 indicators are analysed.

Activities 6.3

1. A computer system that allows different types of geographical data to be linked to a location and displayed in an easily understandable form.

2. First developed by the Canadian government in the 1960s.

3. Cost savings and increased efficiency; Improved decision-making; Better communication; More efficient recordkeeping; The much-improved ability to manage geographically.

4. Examples are: identifying areas liable to flooding; analysing patterns of crime; monitoring weather systems.

Index